need to know?

Decorating

Collins

First published in 2006 by Collins
an imprint of
HarperCollins Publishers
77–85 Fulham Palace Road
London W6 8JB

www.collins.co.uk

09   08   07   06
8   7   6   5   4   3   2   1

A catalogue record for this book is available from
the British Library

Created by **Focus Publishing**, Sevenoaks, Kent
Project editor: Guy Croton
Editor: Vanessa Townsend
Designer: David Etherington
Series design: Mark Thomson
Front cover photograph: © Getty Images/Digital
Vision

The publishers would like to thank the following for
the use of their images: The Rohm and Haas Paint
Quality Institute (www.paintquality.co.uk) p166,
p174, p176, back cover – bottom; Crown Paints
(www.crownpaints.co.uk) p2, p6, p73, p76, p104,
p140, p177, back cover – 2nd from top; The Stencil
Library (Tel: 01661 844844, www.stencil-library.com)
p169, p170, p175, p178 (top).

ISBN-13: 978 0 00 720818 0
ISBN-10: 0 00 720818 9

Colour reproduction by Colourscan, Singapore
Printed and bound by Printing Express Ltd,
Hong Kong

Contents

1 Getting started

In common with other practical pursuits, decorating your house requires a bit of forward planning – not only in respect of the specific decorating you plan to undertake, but also the type of tools and equipment you will need to carry out the task. The last thing you want to have to do is to break off in the middle of a job and run down to the nearest DIY store to buy a tool that you now realize is essential. So, be organized: get everything together before you begin and you won't need to down tools before you even start!

Introduction to decorating

To help the job go off smoothly, before you even wield a paintbrush or rub down woodwork it pays to tidy up the area in which you are going to be working as much as possible – this applies to outside as well as inside tasks.

Before you begin

If you are going to decorate outside, it is important to consider the timing, the weather and the condition of the site. Indoors, you have the not inconsiderable problem of what to do with a room full of furniture and furnishings while you are working. We will examine the various problems associated with both inside and outside decorating jobs.

Outside the house

Plan your work so that you can begin decorating in late summer or early autumn, when the previous warm weather will have dried out the fabric of the building sufficiently.

The best weather for decorating is a warm but overcast day. Avoid painting on rainy days or in direct sunlight, as both rain and hot sun can ruin new paintwork. On a sunny day, follow the sun around the house, so that its warmth will have dried out the night's dew on the woodwork before you apply paint.

It's not a good idea to decorate on windy days, because dust is invariably blown onto the wet paint. In order to settle dust that would otherwise be churned up by your feet, sprinkle water around doors and windows before you start painting.

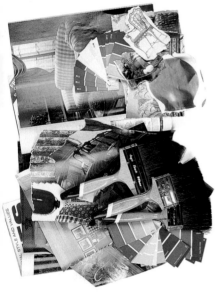

Look through style magazines and colour charts to help you decide on a scheme.

Walk around the house to check there are no obstructions that could slow your progress or cause accidents. Clear away any rubbish, and cut back overhanging foliage from trees and shrubs. Protect plants and paving in the work area with dust sheets; you do not want your well-tended shrubs or newly-laid patio getting splattered with paint or cement.

Inside the house

Before decorating a room, carry out any necessary repairs and, if you use an open fire, have the chimney swept – a soot fall would ruin your new decorations! It pays to clear as much furniture as possible from the room; stack it up in a neighbouring room and group what furniture is left under dustsheets. Take up loose carpets and rugs, then lightly spray water on the floor and sweep up the dust. Protect finished wood flooring, tiled floors and fitted carpets with dust sheets. When painting the skirting, stick wide low-tack masking tape around the perimeter of the floor.

Remove all furnishings, such as pictures and lampshades, and unscrew fingerplates and door handles. Keep the door handle with you in the room, in case you accidentally get shut in.

Means of access

Whether you need to reach guttering or require a simple step-up to paint the living-room ceiling, it is essential to use strong and stable equipment.

This outdoor ladder incorporates a device to prevent the ladder leaning against the guttering or eaves, which may cause damage.

Ladders and scaffolding

Stepladders are essential when decorating indoors. Traditional wooden stepladders are still available, but they have largely been superseded by lightweight aluminium-alloy versions. It is worth having at least one that stands about 2m (6ft 6in) high, so you can reach a ceiling without having to stand on the top step, putting yourself in a dangerous position. A shorter ladder may be more convenient for other jobs; and you can use both, with scaffold boards, to build a platform.

Outdoors, you will need ladders that reach up to the eaves. Double and triple wooden extension ladders are very heavy, so consider metal ones. Some doubles and most triples are operated by a rope and pulley.

To estimate the length of ladder you need, add together the ceiling heights of your house, then add at least 1m (3ft 3in) to the length – to allow for leaning the ladder at an angle and for safe access to a platform.

There are many versions of dual-purpose or even multi-purpose ladders that convert from stepladder to straight ladder. This type is a good compromise.

Sectional scaffold frames can be built up to form towers at any convenient height for decorating inside and out. Broad feet prevent the scaffold sinking into the ground, and adjustable versions allow you to level it.

Towers are ideal for painting a large expanse of wall outdoors. Indoors, smaller platforms bring high ceilings within easy reach.

Working with ladders

More accidents are caused by using ladders unwisely than by faulty equipment. Erect the ladder safely before you climb it; and move it when work is out of reach. Never lean to the side, or you will overbalance. Follow these rules and you will be safe.

How to handle a ladder

Ladders are heavy and unwieldy. Handle them properly to avoid damaging property and to make sure you don't injure yourself.

Carry a ladder upright, not slung across your shoulder. Hold the ladder vertically, bend your knees slightly, then rock the ladder back against your shoulder. Grip one rung lower down

Wooden ladders should have sturdy, hardwood rungs.

must know

When you buy or hire a ladder, bear the following in mind
▶ Wooden ladders should be made from straight-grained timber.
▶ Good-quality wooden ladders have hardwood rungs tenoned through the upright stiles and secured with wedges.
▶ Wooden rungs with reinforcing metal rods stretched under them are safer than ones without.
▶ End caps or foot pads help prevent the ladder from slipping.
▶ Choose a ladder that will enable you to gain access to various parts of the building and will convert to a compact unit for storage.
▶ Rungs of overlapping sections of an extension ladder should align or the gap between rungs might be too small to secure a good foothold.
▶ Choose an extension ladder with a rope and pulley, plus an automatic latch that locks the extension to its rung.
▶ Check that you can buy or hire a range of accessories to fit your make of ladder.
▶ Choose a stepladder with a platform at the top for paint cans.
▶ Wide, flat treads are best and are comfortable to stand on.
▶ Extended stiles give you a handhold at the top of the steps.
▶ Wooden stepladders often have a rope to stop the two halves sliding apart. A better solution used on most metal stepladders is a folding stay that locks in the open position.

while you support the ladder at head height with your other hand, and then straighten your knees.

To erect a ladder, lay it on the ground with its feet against the wall. Raise it to vertical as you walk towards the wall. Pull the feet out from the wall so that the ladder rests at an angle of about 70 degrees: if it extends to 8m (26ft), for example, its feet should be 2m (6ft 6in) – a quarter of its height – from the wall.

Hold an extending ladder upright while raising it to the required height. If it is a heavy ladder, get someone to hold it while you operate the pulley.

Secure the base of the ladder by lashing it to stakes in the ground.

Securing the ladder

If the ground is soft, place a wide board under the ladder's feet; screw a batten across the board to hold the ladder in place. On hard ground, ensure the ladder has anti-slip end caps and lay a sandbag (or a tough polythene bag filled with earth) at the base.

When you extend a ladder, the sections should overlap by at least a quarter of their length. Don't lean the top of the ladder against gutters, soil pipes or drainpipes, as these may give way, and especially not against glass. Anchor the ladder near the top by tying it to a stout timber rail held across the inside of the window frame. Pad the ends with cloth to protect the wall.

It's a good idea to fix ring bolts at regular intervals into the masonry just below the fascia board: this is an excellent way to secure the top of a ladder, as you will have equally good anchor points wherever you choose to position it.

Anchor the ladder to a batten held inside the window frame.

Safety aloft

Never climb higher than four rungs from the top of the ladder or you will not be able to balance properly and there will be no handholds within reach. Avoid slippery footholds by placing a sack or doormat at the foot of the ladder to dry your boots on before you ascend.

Erecting work platforms

Rather than moving the ladder little by little as the decorating progresses, it is more convenient to build a work platform that allows you to tackle a large area without moving the structure.

Improvised platform

Clamp or tie the board to the rungs and use two boards, one on top of the other, if two people need to use the platform at once.

A better arrangement is to use scaffold-tower components to make a mobile platform. One with locking castors is ideal for decorating ceilings.

Decorating in a stairwell

It's not always easy to build a safe platform for decorating in a stairwell. The simplest method is to use a dual-purpose ladder, which can be adjusted to stand evenly on a flight of stairs. Anchor the steps with rope through a couple of large screw eyes fixed to the stair risers; if the stairs are carpeted, the holes

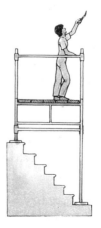

Above: A simple yet safe platform made from stepladders and a scaffold board.

Far left: Use this type of ladder to straddle the stairs and a scaffold board to create a level platform.

Left: Erect a platform with scaffold frames to compensate for the slope of a staircase.

Modern aluminium ladders often feature various accessories to allow them to be used as scaffolding or arranged in a platform layout.

will be concealed. Rest a scaffold board between the ladder and the landing to form a bridge. Screw the board to the landing and tie the other end.

Alternatively, construct a tailor-made platform from ladders and boards to suit your staircase. Make sure the boards and ladders are lashed together securely, and that the ladders cannot slip on the stair treads. If necessary, screw wooden battens to the stairs to prevent the foot of the ladder moving.

Scaffold towers

It is best to erect scaffolding when decorating the outside of a house. Towers made from slot-together frames are available for hire. Heights up to about 9m (30ft) are possible; taller towers require supporting 'outriggers' to prevent them toppling sideways.

Build the lower section of the frame first and level it with adjustable feet before erecting the tower on top.

Erect a proper platform at the top with toe boards all round to prevent tools and materials being knocked off. Extend the framework to provide hand rails all round. Secure the tower by tying it to ring bolts fixed into the masonry, as with ladders.

Some towers incorporate a staircase inside the scaffold frame; floors with trap doors enable you to ascend to the top of the tower. If you cannot hire such a tower, the safest alternative is to use a ladder, but make sure it extends at least 1m (3ft 3in) above the staging, so you can step on and off safely.

Using a ladder, it is difficult to reach windows and walls above an extension. With a scaffold tower, however, you can construct a cantilevered section that rests on the roof of the extension.

Decorating tools

Most home owners collect a fairly extensive kit of tools for decorating their houses or flats. Although traditionalists will want to stick to tried-and-tested tools and to materials of proven reliability, others may prefer to try recent innovations aimed at making the work easier and faster for the home decorator.

Tools for preparation

Whether you're tiling, painting or papering, ensure the surface to which the materials will be applied is sound and clean.

Wallpaper and paint scrapers

The wide stiff blade of a scraper is for removing softened paint or soaked paper. The best scrapers have high-quality steel blades and riveted rosewood handles.

A scraper with a blade 100 to 125mm (4 to 5in) wide is best for stripping wallpaper, while a narrow one, no more than 25mm (1in) wide, is better for removing paint from window frames and doorframes.

Steam wallpaper stripper

To remove wallpaper quickly (especially thick wallcoverings or where there are multi-layers of wallpaper to take off), either buy or hire an electric steam-generating stripper.

Essential decorating tools are wallpaper scrapers, filling knife, combination shavehook and abrasive paper.

All steam strippers work on similar principles, but follow any specific safety instructions that come with your particular machine.

An orbital wallpaper scorer.

Wallpaper scorer and scraper

Running a scorer across a wall punches minute perforations through the paper so that water or steam can penetrate faster.

Filling knife

A filling knife looks like a paint scraper, but has a flexible blade for forcing filler into cracks in timber or plaster.

Mastic guns

Collect all your decorating tools together before you get going.

Permanently flexible non-setting mastic is used to seal joints between materials with different rates of expansion. You can buy mastic that you squeeze direct from a plastic tube, but it's easier with a cartridge clipped into a spring-loaded gun.

Abrasives

Wet-and-dry abrasive paper is used to smooth new paintwork or varnish before applying the final coat. Dip a piece in water and rub the paintwork until a slurry of paint and water forms. Wipe with a cloth before it dries and rinse the paper clean.

Paintbrushes

Some paintbrushes are made from natural animal hair. Hog bristle is the best, but it is often mixed with inferior horsehair or oxhair. Synthetic-bristle brushes are generally the least expensive and are quite adequate for the home decorator.

Cleaning paintbrushes

▶ **Water-based paints** As soon as you finish, wash the bristles with warm soapy water, working the paint out of the roots. Then rinse the brush in clean water and shake out the excess. Smooth the bristles and slip an elastic band round their tips to hold the shape of the filling while it is drying.

▶ **Solvent-based paints** If you're using solvent-based paints, suspend the brush overnight in enough water covering the bristles, then blot with kitchen paper before resuming painting. When you have finished, brush out excess paint onto newspaper, then flex the bristles in a bowl of thinners.

▶ **Hardened paint** If paint has hardened on a brush, soften it by soaking the bristles in brush cleaner or paint stripper if very stubborn. Then wash out with hot water.

Paint rollers

A paint roller (right) is the ideal tool for painting a large area of wall or ceiling quickly.

Paint spraying equipment

Spraying is so fast and efficient that it's worth considering when you are planning to paint the outside walls of a building. Plan to work on a dry and windless day and allow time to mask off windows, doors and pipework. Follow the handling instructions supplied with the equipment; and if you are new to the work, practise beforehand on an inconspicuous section of wall.

Choosing a brush
The bristles of a good brush – the 'filling' – are densely packed. When you fan them with your fingers they should spring back into shape immediately. Flex the tip of the brush against your hand to see if any bristles work loose. Even a good brush will shed a few bristles at first, but never clumps of bristles. The ferrule should be fixed firmly to the handle.

Paperhanger's tools

Pasting table

You can paste wallcoverings on any flat surface, but a purpose-made pasting table is a much better idea. It is only 25mm (1in) wider than a standard roll of wallpaper, which makes it easier to spread paste without getting it onto the worktop.

Paperhanger's brush

This is used for smoothing wallcoverings onto a wall or ceiling. Its bristles should be soft, so as not to damage delicate paper, but springy enough to squeeze out air bubbles and excess paste.

Tiling tools

Most tiling tools are for applying ceramic wall and floor tiles.

Spirit level

You will need a spirit level for setting up temporary battens in order to align a field of tiles both horizontally and vertically.

Tile cutter

A tile cutter has either a pointed tungsten-carbide tip or a steel wheel (similar to a glass cutter's) for scoring the glazed surface of ceramic tiles.

Grout spreader or rubber float

The spreader has a hard-rubber blade mounted in a plastic handle. The float looks similar to a wooden float but has a rubber sole. Both are used for grouting between ceramic tiles.

Nibblers

To snap a very narrow strip off a ceramic tile, score the line with a tile cutter then break off the waste bit by bit with tile nibblers. These resemble pincers but have sharper jaws that open when you relax your grip on the spring-loaded handles.

Colour schemes

Developing a sense of the 'right' colour isn't the same as learning to paint a door or hang wallpaper. There are no 'rules' as such, but there are guidelines that will help.

Colour tips

In magazine articles on interior design and colour selection, you will find terms such as 'harmony' and 'contrast'; colours are described as tints or shades, and as cool or warm. These terms form a basis for developing a colour scheme. By considering colours as the spokes of a wheel, you will see how they relate to each other.

A colour wheel groups warm and cool colours on opposite sides of the wheel.

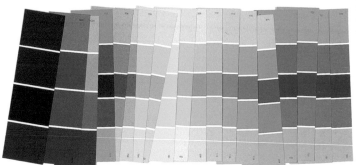

A colour palette showing warm and cool colours in order from left to right.

Warm and cool colours

The wheel groups colours with similar characteristics. On one side are the warm red and yellow combinations, colours we associate with fire and sunlight. A room decorated with warm colours feels cosy or exciting, depending on the intensity of the colours used. Cool colours are grouped on the opposite side of the wheel. Blues and greens suggest vegetation, water and sky, and create a relaxed airy feeling when used together.

The use of colour

Our eyes perceive colours and tones in such a way that it is possible to create optical illusions that apparently change the dimensions of a room. Warm colours appear to advance – so a room painted brown, red or orange, for example, will give the impression of being smaller than the same room decorated in cool colours, such as blues and greens, which have a tendency to recede.

Tone can be used to modify or reinforce the required illusion. Dark tones – even when you are using cool colours – will advance, while pale tones will open up a space visually.

The same qualities of colour and tone will change the proportions of a space. Adjusting the height of a ceiling is an obvious example. If you paint a ceiling a darker tone than the walls, it will appear lower, so lighter colours generally work better in dormer windows, alcoves and so on, making them appear higher than they are in reality. If you make a floor too dark, it is almost as if the room is squeezed between the two walls. A long, narrow passageway will feel less claustrophobic if you push out the walls by decorating them with pale, cool colours.

Using linear pattern is yet another way to alter the perception of space. Vertically striped wallpaper or woodstrip panelling on the walls will counteract the effect of a low ceiling. Venetian blinds make windows seem wider, and stripped wooden floors are stretched in the direction of the boards. Any large-scale pattern draws attention to itself and – in the same way as warm, dark colours – will advance, while from a distance small patterns appear as an overall texture and so have less effect.

The light-reflecting sheen of silk vinyl or satin emulsion makes the most of natural light.

want to know more?

Take it to the next level...

▶ **Safety when painting** 78
▶ **Painting exterior masonry** 79
▶ **Papering stairwells** 118–19
▶ **Choosing tiles** 126–7
▶ **Decorating with paint effects** 176

Other sources
▶ Consult the painting and decorating people at your local DIY store – they are normally happy to help.
▶ Watch DIY and home makeover programmes on television to learn handy tips and get you in the mood for doing your own decorating.
▶ Try out DIY and painting and decorating websites such as www.paintquality.co.uk for ideas and current information (see also the list of websites in the 'Need to know more?' section on page 188 of this book).
▶ For more in-depth information about getting started in home decorating, read Collins' bestselling *Complete DIY Manual* by Albert Jackson and David Day.

2 General preparation

There is an old adage in the folklore of DIY which says that any job you do will only ever be as good as the preparation that went into it. Never is this more true than when it comes to painting and decorating. If you don't do the general preparation properly, once you finish the job it will not look as good as you expected and you will spend ages cursing yourself for not having taken sufficient time and trouble at the outset! Remember, preparation is all...

Preparation and priming

Thorough preparation of all surfaces is a vital first step in redecorating. If you neglect this stage, subsequent finishes may be rejected. Preparation means removing dirt, grease and loose or flaking finishes, as well as repairing serious deterioration such as cracks, holes, corrosion and decay.

Sealing surfaces

It is not only old surfaces that need attention. New timber must be sealed for protection, and priming is necessary to ensure a surface is in a suitable condition to accept its finish. Consult the chart opposite for details of primers and sealers for all the materials you are likely to encounter in and around the home.

Types of primer and sealer

Stabilizing primer Used to bind powdery or flaky materials. A clear or white liquid.

Wood primer Standard solvent-based pink or white primer prevents other coats of paint soaking in.

Acrylic wood primer Fast-drying water-based primer.

Aluminium wood primer Used to seal oily hardwoods and resinous softwoods.

General-purpose primer Seals porous building materials and covers patchy walls and ceilings. Some multi-purpose primers are suitable for wood, metal and plaster.

Metal primers Essential to prevent corrosion in metals and to provide a key for paint. Special rust-inhibitive primers treat rust and prevent its recurrence.

PVA bonding agent A general-purpose liquid adhesive for many building materials. An excellent primer and sealer when diluted, even for bituminous paints.

Water repellent A liquid used for sealing masonry against water penetration.

Alkali-resistant primer Prevents alkali content of some materials attacking oil paints.

Aluminium spirit-based sealer Helps obliterate materials likely to 'bleed' through subsequent coatings. Good over bituminous paints, creosote and metallic paints.

Stain sealer Permanently seals problem stains such as nicotine, water, soot, crayon, lipstick and ballpoint pen.

Panel-system primer Provides better adhesion for masonry paints applied to building boards. Used with polyester scrim, it can be used to reinforce repaired cracks in exterior render.

Primers and sealers: Suitability, drying time and coverage

	Stabilizing primer	Wood primer	Acrylic wood primer	Aluminium wood primer	General-purpose primer	Zinc-phosphate primer	Fast-drying metal primer	Rust-inhibitive primer	PVA bonding agent	Water repellent	Alkali-resistant primer	Aluminium spirit-based sealer	Stain sealer	Panel-system primer
SUITABLE FOR														
Brick	•				•				•	•	•			
Stone	•				•				•	•	•			
Cement rendering	•				•				•	•	•			•
Concrete	•				•				•	•	•			
Plaster	•				•				•				•	
Plasterboard	•				•						•		•	
Distemper	•													
Limewash	•													
Cement paint	•													
Bitumen-based paints									•			•		
Asbestos cement	•				•				•		•			
Soft/hardwoods		•	•	•	•									
Oily hardwoods				•										
Chipboard		•	•	•	•									•
Hardboard		•	•	•	•									•
Plywood		•	•	•	•									•
Creosoted timber				•									•	
Absorbent fibre boards	•										•			
Ferrous metals (inside)						•		•						
Ferrous metals (outside)						•		•						
Galvanized metal						•	•							
Aluminium						•	•							
DRYING TIME: HOURS														
Touch-dry	3	4-6	0.5	4-6	4-6	4	0.5	2	3	1	4	0.25	2-3	-
Recoatable	16	16	2	16	16	16	6	6	16	16	16	1	6-8	24
COVERAGE (sq m per litre)														
Brick	6	12	12	13	12	13	8	8	9	3-6	10	4	18	6
Brick	7	10	1-	11	9	10	-	6	7	2-3	7	3	-	3

Cleaning masonry

Before you decorate the outside of your house, check the condition of the brick and stonework, and carry out any necessary repairs.

Stained brickwork

Treating new masonry

New brickwork or stonework should be left for about three months before any further treatment is considered.

White powdery deposits – called efflorescence – may come to the surface over this period, but brush them off with a stiff-bristle brush (see below). New masonry should be weatherproof and so should require no further treatment.

Cleaning off unsightly mould

The spread of moulds and lichens depends on damp conditions, so it is not a good sign when they occur naturally on the walls of your house. Try to identify the source of the problem before treating the growth. For example, try cutting back overhanging trees or adjacent shrubs to increase ventilation to the wall.

Make sure the damp-proof course (DPC) is working adequately and is not being bridged by piled earth or debris.

Cracked or corroded rainwater pipes leaking onto the wall are another common cause. Feel behind the pipe with your fingers or slip a hand mirror behind it to see if there's a leak.

Organic growth

Removing efflorescence from masonry

Soluble salts within building materials such as cement, brick and stone gradually migrate to the surface, along with the moisture, as a wall dries out. The result is a white crystalline deposit called efflorescence.

The same condition can occur on old masonry if it is subjected to more than average moisture. Simply brush the

Efflorescence

deposit from the wall regularly, with a dry stiff-bristle brush or coarse sacking, until the crystals cease to form. Don't attempt to wash off the crystals – they will merely dissolve in the water and soak back into the wall. Don't decorate a wall that is still efflorescing, as this is a sign that it is still damp.

Masonry paints and clear sealants that let the wall breathe are not affected by the alkali content of the masonry, so can be used without applying a primer. If you plan to use solvent-based (oil) paint, coat the wall first with an alkali-resistant primer.

Cleaning masonry

You can often spruce up old masonry by washing off surface grime with water. Strong solvents will harm certain types of stone, so ask an experienced local builder before applying anything other than water.

Washing the wall

Starting at the top, play a hose gently onto the masonry while you scrub it with a stiff-bristle brush (1). Scrub heavy deposits with half a cup of ammonia added to a bucket of water, then rinse again. Avoid soaking brick or stone when a frost is forecast.

Stripping spilled paint

To remove a patch of spilled paint, use a proprietary paint stripper. Follow the manufacturer's recommendations, and wear gloves and goggles.

Stipple the stripper onto the rough texture (2). Leave for about 10 minutes, then remove the paint with a scraper. Gently scrub the residue out of deeper crevices with a stiff-bristle brush and water. Then rinse the wall with clean water.

1 Remove dirt and dust by washing.

2 Stipple paint stripper onto wall.

Repointing masonry

A combination of frost action and erosion tends to break down the mortar pointing of brickwork and stonework. The mortar eventually falls out, exposing the open joints to wind and rain, which drive dampness through the wall to the inside. Replacing defective pointing is a straightforward but time-consuming task.

must know

Mortar dyes

Liquid or powder additives are available for changing the colour of mortar to match existing pointing. Colour matching is difficult, and smears can stain the bricks permanently.

Applying the mortar

Rake out the old pointing with a thin wooden lath to a depth of about 12mm (½in). Use a cold chisel, or a special plugging chisel, and a club hammer to dislodge sections that are firmly embedded, then brush out the joints with a stiff-bristle brush.

Spray the wall with water, to make sure the bricks or stones will not absorb too much moisture from the fresh mortar. Mix up some mortar in a bucket and transfer it to a hawk. If you are mixing your own mortar, use the proportions 1 part cement : 1 part lime : 6 parts builders' sand.

Pick up a small sausage of mortar on the back of a pointing trowel and push it firmly into the upright joints. This can be difficult to do without the mortar dropping off, so hold the hawk under each joint to catch it. Try not to smear the face of the bricks with mortar, as it will stain. Do the same for horizontal joints. The actual shape of the pointing is not vital at this stage.

Once the mortar is firm enough to retain a thumbprint, it is ready for shaping. Because it is important that you shape the joints at exactly the right moment, you may have to point the work in stages in order to complete the wall. Shape the joints to match existing brickwork (see opposite) or choose a profile suitable for the prevailing weather conditions in your area.

Once you have shaped the joints, wait until the pointing has almost hardened, then brush the wall to remove traces of surplus mortar from the surface of the masonry.

Shaping the mortar joints

The joints shown here are commonly used for brickwork. Flush or rubbed joints are best for most stonework. Leave the pointing of dressed-stone ashlar blocks to an expert.

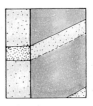

Flush joint

Flush joints

This is the easiest profile to produce. Scrape the mortar flush, using the edge of your trowel, then stipple the joints with a stiff-bristle brush to expose the sand aggregate.

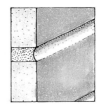

Rubbed joint

Rubbed (concave) joints

This joint is ideal for an old wall with bricks that are not of sufficiently good quality to take a crisp joint. Bricklayers make a rubbed joint using a jointer, a tool shaped like a sled runner with a handle. Flush the mortar, then drag the tool along the joints. Finish the vertical joints, then shape the horizontals. Finally, stipple the joints with a brush so that they look weathered.

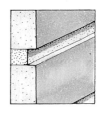

Raked joint

Raked joints

A raked joint is used to emphasize the bonding pattern of a brick wall. It is not suitable for an exposed site where the wall takes a lot of weathering. Rake out the new joints to a depth of about 6mm (¼in), and then compress the mortar by smoothing it lightly with a lath or a piece of rounded dowel rod.

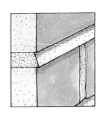

Weatherstruck joint

Weatherstruck joints

The sloping profile is intended to shed rainwater from the wall. Shape the mortar with the edge of a pointing trowel. Start with the vertical joints, sloping them either to the right or to the left (but be consistent). Then shape the horizontal joints, allowing the mortar to spill out at the base of each joint. Finish the joint by cutting off the excess mortar with a Frenchman, a tool with a narrow blade with the tip bent at 90 degrees. Use a wooden batten to guide the Frenchman along the joints.

Use a Frenchman to trim weatherstruck joints.

Repairing masonry

Cracked masonry may simply be the result of cement-rich mortar being unable to absorb slight movements within the building. However, it could also be a sign of a more serious problem, such as subsiding foundations. Don't just ignore the symptoms, but investigate immediately and put the necessary repairs in hand.

Cracks may follow pointing only.

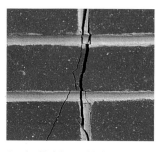

Cracked bricks could signify serious faults.

must know

Priming for painting
Brickwork will only need to be primed if it is showing signs of efflorescence or spalling. An alkali-resistant primer will guard against the former.

Filling cracked masonry

Cracked mortar can be removed and repointed in the normal way, but a crack that splits the bricks cannot be repaired neatly, and the damaged masonry should be replaced by a builder.

Cracks across a painted wall can be filled with mortar mixed with a little PVA bonding agent to help it stick. Wet the damaged masonry with a hose to encourage the mortar to flow deeply into the crack.

Waterproofing masonry

Colourless water-repellent fluids are intended to make masonry impervious to water without colouring it or stopping it from breathing.

Make good any cracks in bricks or pointing and remove organic growth, then allow the wall to dry.

The fumes from water-repellent fluid can be dangerous if inhaled, so wear a proper respirator, as well as eye protectors.

Apply the fluid generously with a large paintbrush, from the bottom up, and stipple it into the joints. Apply a second coat once the first has been absorbed.

If you need to treat a whole house, it may be worth hiring a company that can spray the sealant.

Repairing render

Brickwork is sometimes clad with a smooth or roughcast cement-based render, both for improved weatherproofing and to provide a decorative finish. However, it is susceptible to damp and frost, which can cause cracking, bulging and staining.

Repairing defects

Before you repair cracked render, have a builder check the wall for any structural faults that may have contributed to the problem.

You can ignore fine hairline cracks if you intend to paint the wall with a reinforced masonry paint, but rake out larger cracks with a cold chisel. Dampen them with water and fill flush with a cement-based exterior filler. Fill any major cracks with a render made of 1 part cement, 2 parts lime and 9 parts builder's sand, plus a little PVA bonding agent to help it stick to the wall.

Bulges normally indicate that the cladding has parted from the masonry. Tap the wall gently with a wooden mallet to find the extent of these hollow areas, then hack off the material to sound edges. Use a bolster chisel to undercut the perimeter of each hole except for the bottom edge, which should be left square, so that it does not collect water.

Brush out the debris, then apply a coat of PVA bonding agent. When tacky, trowel on a layer of 1 : 1 : 6 render, 12mm (½in) thick, using plasterer's sand. Leave to set firm, then scratch it to form a key.

Next day, fill flush with a weaker mix (1 : 1 : 9) and smooth the surface with a wooden float, using circular strokes.

watch out!

Preparation
Before you redecorate a rendered wall, make good any damage and clean off surface dirt, mould growth and flaky material, in order to achieve a long-lasting finish.

Cracked render allows moisture to penetrate.

Painted masonry

Painted masonry inside the house is usually in fairly good order, and apart from a good wash-down to remove dust and grease and a light sanding to give a key for the new finish, there is little else you need to do. Outside, however, it's a different matter.

A painted wall in need of restoration.

A chalky surface needs stabilizing.

Strip flaky paintwork to a sound surface.

Outside masonry

Exterior surfaces, subjected to extremes of heat, cold and rain, are likely to be affected to some degree by stains, flaking and chalkiness.

Curing a chalky surface

Rub the palm of your hand lightly over the surface of the wall to see if it is chalky. If the paint rubs off as a powdery deposit, treat the wall before you redecorate.

Brush the surface with a stiff-bristle brush, then paint the whole wall liberally with a stabilizing primer to bind the chalky surface so that paint will adhere to it. Use a white stabilizing primer, which can also serve as an undercoat. Clean splashes of the fluid from surrounding woodwork with white spirit.

If the wall is very dusty, apply a second coat after about 16 hours. Wait a further 16 hours before applying paint.

Dealing with flaky paint

Poor surface preparation or incompatible paint and preparatory treatments are common causes of flaky paintwork. Damp walls will also cause flaking, so cure the damp and let the wall dry out before further treatment.

A new coat of paint will not bind to a flaky surface, so this needs to be remedied before you start painting. Use a paint scraper and stiff-bristle brush to remove all loose material. Coarse glasspaper should finish the job or at least feather the edges of any stubborn patches. Stabilize the surface as for chalky walls before repainting.

Treating a stained chimney

If the outlines of brick courses show up as brown staining on a painted chimney stack, this is caused by a breakdown of the internal rendering, or 'pargeting', of the chimney. Defective pargeting allows tar deposits to migrate through the mortar joints to the outer paintwork. To solve this, first fit a flue liner in the chimney, then treat the brown stains with an aluminium spirit-based sealer before applying a fresh coat of paint.

Treat tar stains with aluminium sealer.

Stripping painted masonry

In the past even sound brickwork was painted to 'brighten up' a house. In some areas of the country where painted masonry is traditional, there is every reason to continue with the practice. Indeed, houses with soft, inferior brickwork were frequently painted when they were built to protect them from the weather. However, one painted house in an otherwise natural-brick terrace tends to spoil the whole row; and painting one half of a pair of semi-detached houses has an equally undesirable effect.

Chimney stained by tar deposits from the flue.

Restoring painted brickwork to its natural condition is not an easy task. It is generally a messy business, involving the use of toxic materials that have to be handled with care and disposed of safely. Getting the masonry entirely clean demands considerable experience. Therefore, it is advisable to hire professionals to do the work for you.

To determine whether the outcome is likely to be successful, ask the company you are thinking of hiring to strip an inconspicuous patch of masonry, using the chemicals they recommend for the job. The results may indicate that it is better to repaint – in which case, choose a good-quality masonry paint that will let moisture within the walls evaporate.

Repairing concrete

Concrete suffers from the effects of damp – spalling and efflorescence – and related defects, such as cracking and crumbling. Repairs can usually be made in the same way as for brickwork and render.

must know

Binding dusty concrete
Concrete is trowelled when it is laid, to give it a flat finish. If the trowelling is overdone, cement is brought to the surface; and when the concrete dries out, this thin layer begins to break up, producing a loose, dusty surface. Though not always applicable, it is generally recommended that you paint on a concrete-floor sealer before applying decorative finishes. Treat a dusty concrete wall with stabilizing primer.

Sealing concrete

New concrete has a high alkali content, so efflorescence can develop on the surface as it dries. Use only water-thinnable paint until the concrete is completely dry. When treating efflorescence on concrete, follow the procedure recommended for brickwork. A porous concrete wall should be waterproofed with a clear sealant on the exterior.

Cleaning dirty concrete

You can scrub dirty concrete with water (as for brickwork); but when a concrete drive or garage floor is stained with patches of oil or grease, you will need to apply a proprietary oil-and-grease remover. Brush on the solution liberally, then scrub the surface with a stiff-bristle brush. Rinse off with clean water. Soak up fresh oil spillages immediately with dry sand or sawdust to prevent them becoming permanent stains.

Repairing cracks and holes

Rake out and brush away loose debris from cracks and holes in concrete. If the crack is less than 6mm (¼in) wide, open it up a little so it will accept a filling (see opposite). To fill a hole in concrete, add a fine aggregate such as gravel to a sand-and-cement mix. Make sure the fresh concrete sticks in shallow depressions by priming the damaged surface with 3 parts bonding agent : 1 part water. When the primed surface is tacky, trowel in the concrete and smooth it.

Treating spalled concrete

When concrete breaks up, or spalls, due to the action of frost, the process is accelerated as steel reinforcement is exposed and begins to corrode. Fill the concrete as described opposite, but paint the metalwork first with a rust-inhibitive primer.

Levelling floors

An uneven or pitted concrete floor must be made level before you apply any form of floorcovering. You can do this fairly easily yourself using a proprietary self-levelling compound, but ensure the surface is dry before proceeding.

Spalling concrete.

Testing for damp

If you suspect a concrete floor is damp, test it by laying a small piece of polythene on the concrete and sealing it with self-adhesive parcel tape. After one or two days, inspect it for any traces of moisture on the underside. If the test shows signs of moisture, apply three coats of heavy-duty, moisture-cured polyurethane sealant. No longer than four hours should elapse between coats. The floor should be as dry as possible, so that it is porous enough for the first coat to penetrate.

Before applying a self-levelling compound, lightly scatter dry sand over the last coat of sealant while it is still wet. Allow it to harden for three days, then brush off loose residual sand.

Before you fill a narrow crack, open it up and undercut the edges using a cold chisel.

Spread the compound with a trowel.

Applying a self-levelling compound

Self-levelling compound is supplied as a powder that you mix with water. Having made sure the floor is clean and free from damp, pour some of the compound in the corner furthest from the door. Spread the compound with a trowel until it is about 3mm (⅛in) thick, then leave it to seek its own level. Continue across the floor until the entire surface is covered. Leave the compound to harden for a few days before laying a permanent floorcovering.

Preparing plasterwork

A cracked, unstable or damp-damaged plaster surface will spoil any paint that is applied to it, so be sure to remedy any problems before you start decorating.

Prime new plaster.

Preparing new plaster

Before you decorate new plaster, wait to see if any efflorescence forms on the surface. Keep wiping it off with dry sacking until it ceases to appear.

Once fresh plaster is dry, you can stick ceramic tiles on the wall, but always leave it for about six months before decorating with wallpaper or any paint other than new-plaster emulsion. Even then, you should use an alkali-resistant primer first if you are applying solvent-based paints. Size new absorbent plaster before hanging wallpaper, or the water will be sucked too quickly from the paste, and the paper will simply peel off the wall. If you are hanging a vinyl wallcovering, make sure the size contains fungicide.

Preparing old plaster

Apart from filling minor defects (see box opposite) and dusting down, old dry plaster in good condition needs no further preparation. If the wall is patchy, apply a general-purpose primer. If the surface is friable, apply a stabilizing solution before decorating.

Preparing plasterboard

Fill all joints between newly fixed plasterboard; then, whether you are painting or papering, daub all nail heads with zinc-phosphate primer.

Before you paint plasterboard with solvent-based paint, prime the surface with one coat of general-purpose primer.

Before hanging wallcoverings, seal plasterboard with a general-purpose primer thinned with white spirit. After 48 hours, apply a coat of size.

Preparing painted plaster

Wash sound paintwork with sugar soap. Use medium-grade wet-and-dry abrasive paper, with water, to key the surface of gloss paint.

If the ceiling is stained by smoke and nicotine, prime it with a proprietary stain sealer. Sealers are sold in aerosol cans for treating isolated stains. You can use the stain sealer as the final coat or paint over it with solvent-based paints or emulsions. If you want to hang wallcoverings on oil paint, key then size the wall. Cross-line the wall with lining paper before hanging a heavy embossed wallpaper.

Remove flaking paint with a scraper or stiff-bristle brush. Feather off the edges of the paintwork with wet-and-dry abrasive paper, then treat the bare plaster patches with a general-purpose primer. Apply stabilizing primer if the paint is friable.

You can apply ceramic tiles over sound paintwork. If there is any loose material, remove it first.

Plaster fillers

Interior filler Comes ready-mixed in tubs or as a powder for mixing to a stiff paste with water.

Deep-repair filler Ready-mixed lightweight fillers can be used to fill holes and gaps up to 20mm (¾in) deep without slumping. They are ideal for ceiling repairs.

Fast-setting filler Sold in tube dispensers; perfect for minor repairs and set firm in 10 to 20 minutes.

Flexible acrylic fillers Good for filling gaps between plaster and woodwork. When smoothed with a damp cloth, these gun-applied fillers can be overpainted in one hour. No sanding is required.

Expanding foam Fill large irregular gaps and cavities with expanding polyurethane foam from an aerosol. Finish the job with cellulose or deep-repair fillers.

Repair plasters Make more-extensive repairs with easy-to-use, slow-drying repair plasters.

Patching plasterwork

If you are painting with emulsion, then even hairline cracks must be filled. With larger holes and blemishes, there are a number of methods you can use to patch up the plasterwork.

Dampen the crack.

Press filler into crack.

Filling cracks and holes

Special flexible emulsions and textured paints are designed to cover hairline cracks, but larger cracks, dents and holes will reappear in a short time if they are not filled adequately.

Rake loose material from a crack, using a wallpaper scraper. Undercut the edges of larger cracks to provide a key for the filling. Use a paintbrush to dampen the crack, then press in cellulose filler with a filling knife. Drag the blade across the crack to force the filler in, then draw it along the crack to smooth the filler. Leave the filler standing slightly proud of the surface, ready for rubbing down with abrasive paper.

Fill shallow cracks in one go. But in deep cracks build up the filler in stages, letting each application set before adding more. Alternatively, switch to a deep-repair filler.

Patching a lath-and-plaster wall

In older houses, ceilings and some internal walls are clad with slim strips of wood (laths), which are a base for the plaster.

If the laths are intact, fill holes in the plaster with cellulose filler or repair plaster. If some laths are broken, reinforce the repair with a piece of fine expanded-metal mesh. Rake out loose plaster and undercut the edge of the hole with a bolster chisel. Use tinsnips to cut the metal mesh slightly larger than the shape of the hole (1). The mesh is flexible, so bend it to tuck the edge behind the sound plaster all round (2). Flatten the mesh against the laths with light taps from a hammer; if possible, staple the mesh to a wall stud to hold it in place (3). For papering and tiling, patch the hole with one-coat repair plaster (4). Finish with a thin coat of skimming repair plaster.

1 Cut with tinsnips. **2 Tuck mesh into hole.** **3 Staple mesh to stud.** **4 Trowel on plaster.**

Patching larger holes in plasterboard

A large hole punched through a plasterboard wall or ceiling cannot be patched using with wet plaster only. Using a sharp craft knife and a straightedge, cut back the damaged board to the nearest studs or joists at each side of the hole. Cut a new panel of plasterboard to fit snugly within the hole and nail it to the joists or studs, using galvanized plasterboard nails. Brush on a generous coat of skimming repair plaster and smooth it over the wall with a plasterer's trowel.

Large holes cannot be patched with wet plaster.

Preparing wallcoverings

It's always preferable to strip a previously papered surface before hanging a new wallcovering. However, if the paper is perfectly sound, you can paint it with emulsion or solvent-based paints (though this will make it more difficult to remove in the future).

Hanging lining paper.

Preparing the walls

Inspect the wall surfaces for cracks, holes and any loose plaster, and make any necessary repairs. Older houses are bound to have had plaster repairs over the years and this will make the wall surface extremely uneven.

Lining paper

It is therefore best to hang lining paper, to prevent defects showing through your chosen wallpaper. Hang lining paper horizontally, otherwise joints may coincide with the top covering of wallpaper.

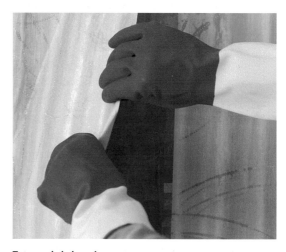

Try to strip in lengths.

Stripping wallpaper

Strip off any existing wallcovering. Do not attempt to get the paper off without thoroughly wetting it first, unless it is a vinyl paper. If it is vinyl, then peel away the top vinyl layer leaving the backing paper on the wall. This then needs to be wetted and stripped off.

It's easier with a steam stripper.

For most wallcoverings, score lines in the paper to break the surface. This will allow the water, or steam, you are going to apply to soak into the backing paper and effectively dissolve the adhesive.

Having scored the paper (proprietary scoring tools, such as orbital sanders, can be found in DIY stores), fill a bucket with warm to hot water and add some washing up liquid to the water. This helps to dissolve the wallpaper adhesive and makes life a lot easier in most circumstances. Wet the paper, using a sponge, leave to soak in for about half an hour, then repeat the soaking. Then using a wallpaper scraper, remove the wallcovering, being careful not to damage the plaster underneath.

Orbital sanders score wallpaper.

Hiring or buying a wallpaper steam stripper will speed up the scraping process and help with really stubborn jobs – for instance, if there are several layers of wallpaper on the surface. However, do not add washing up liquid to the water reservoir!

When the paper has been stripped, wash the walls down with water to remove all traces of paste.

Sizing

Size a plaster wall to prevent loss of adhesion by absorbing the water from the paste. It also makes the wall slippery, which helps when positioning each length of wallpaper. Brush size on to the wall and leave to dry for a short time before hanging the paper.

Carefully remove the old paper.

Preparing woodwork

The wooden joinery in our homes often needs redecorating long before any other part of the house, particularly the exterior of windows and doors, bargeboards and fascias.

Problems with wood

Wood tends to swell when it becomes moist, then shrinks again when the sun or central heating dries it out. Paint won't adhere for long under these conditions, nor will any other finish. Wood is also vulnerable to woodworm and various forms of rot caused primarily by damp, so careful preparation is essential to preserve most types of timber.

Preparing new joinery for painting

New joinery is often primed at the factory, but check that the primer is in good condition before you start work. If the primer is satisfactory, rub it down lightly with fine-grade abrasive paper, dust it off, then apply a second coat of wood primer to areas that will be inaccessible after installation. Don't leave the timber uncovered outside, as primer is not sufficient protection against prolonged exposure to the weather.

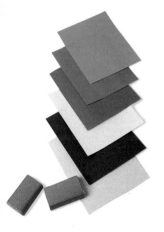

Abrasive paper is graded according to its fineness.

Make sure unprimed timber is dry, then sand the surface in the direction of the grain, using fine-grade sandpaper. Once you have removed all raised grain and lightly rounded any sharp edges, dust the wood down. Finally, rub it over with a rag moistened with white spirit.

Paint bare softwood with a solvent-based wood primer or a quick-drying water-thinned acrylic primer. Apply either primer liberally, taking care to work it well into the joints and, particularly, into the end grain. Apply at least two coats.

Wash oily hardwoods with white spirit immediately prior to priming with an aluminium primer. Use standard wood primers for other hardwoods, thinning them slightly to encourage penetration into the grain.

When the primer is dry, fill open-grained timber with a fine surface filler. Use a piece of coarse cloth to rub it well into the wood with circular strokes followed by parallel strokes in the direction of the grain. When dry, rub down with a fine abrasive paper to a smooth finish.

Fill larger holes, open joints, cracks and other imperfections with flexible interior or exterior wood filler. Press filler into the holes with a filling knife, leaving it slightly proud of the surface so that it can be sanded flush with fine-grade abrasive paper once it has set. Dust down ready for painting.

Clear finishes

There is usually no need to apply knotting when you intend to finish the timber with a clear varnish or lacquer. However, for very resinous timbers, apply white (milky) knotting, which prevents the resin from oozing out of the wood and spoiling the ultimate finish.

Sand wood in the direction of the grain using progressively finer grades of abrasive paper, then seal with a slightly thinned coat of the intended finish.

If the wood is in contact with the ground or in proximity to previous outbreaks of dry rot, treat it first with a liberal wash of clear timber preserver.

Cellulose filler would show through a clear finish, so use a proprietary stopper to fill imperfections. Stoppers are thick pastes made in a range of colours to suit the type of timber. As stoppers can be either oil- or water-based, make sure you use a similar-based dye. Where possible, use an oil-based stopper outside. Stoppers are generally harder than cellulose fillers, so don't overfill blemishes or you will be ages rubbing it down.

Sand along the grain with abrasive paper.

Man-made boards

Versatile and relatively inexpensive, man-made boards are used extensively in the home – typically for shelving, levelling floors, cladding walls and building units for the kitchen or bedroom.

Preparing man-made boards for decoration

Wallboards such as plywood, MDF, chipboard, blockboard, hardboard and softboard are all made from wood, but they must be prepared differently from natural timber. Their finish varies according to the quality of the board: some are compact and smooth, and may even be presealed ready for painting; others must be filled and sanded before you can get a really smooth finish.

1 Plywood, 2 Blockboard, 3 Chipboard,
4 Medium-density fibreboard (MDF),
5 Hardboard back, 6 Hardboard face,
7 Soft fibreboard

As a rough guide, no primer will be required when using acrylic paints, other than a sealing coat of the paint itself, slightly thinned with water. However, any nail or screw heads must be driven below the surface and coated with zinc-phosphate primer to prevent rust stains.

Apply one coat of panel-system primer before painting building boards with masonry paint. If you are using solvent-based paint, prime the boards first with a general-purpose primer or, for porous softboard, a stabilizing primer. Where possible, you should prime both sides of the board. If the boards are presealed, you can apply undercoat directly to the surface.

Bleaching wood

Unevenly coloured or stained board and timber can be bleached before the application of wood dyes and polishes. To avoid a light patch in place of the discoloration, try to bleach the entire area rather than isolated spots.

Using two-part bleach

To use a proprietary two-part wood bleach, brush one part onto the wood and apply the second part over the first, 5 to 10 minutes later. When the bleach is dry, or as soon as the wood is the required colour, neutralize the bleach with a weak acetic-acid solution consisting of a teaspoon of white vinegar in a pint of water.

Put the wood aside for about three days, then sand down the raised grain.

Safety precautions

Wood bleach is a dangerous substance that must be handled with care and stored in the dark, out of the reach of children.

▶ Wear protective gloves, goggles and an apron.
▶ Wear a face mask when sanding bleached wood.
▶ Ensure that ventilation is adequate or work outside.
▶ Have a supply of water handy, in case you splash yourself with bleach.
▶ If you get bleach in your eyes, rinse them thoroughly with running water and see a doctor.
▶ Never mix both parts of the bleach except on the wood, and always apply them with separate white-fibre or nylon brushes.
▶ Discard unused bleach.

Use a paintbrush to apply two-part bleach to stained wood. Leave it until the discoloration has disappeared, then wash off with diluted vinegar.

Sanding a wooden floor

You can turn an unsightly stained and dirty wood floor into an attractive feature by sanding it smooth and clean with hired equipment. Although straightforward, the job is laborious, dusty and extremely noisy.

Lift whole floorboards up using a bolster chisel.

Repairing floorboards

Before you start sanding, examine your floorboards carefully for signs of woodworm infestation. If necessary, have the boards and the joists below treated with a woodworm fluid.

Replace any boards that have more than a few holes in them. If you discover dry or wet rot when you lift up a floorboard, have it treated straightaway.

Look for boards that have been lifted previously by electricians and plumbers. Replace any that are split, too short or badly jointed. Try to find second-hand boards to match the rest of the floor.

A raised nail head will rip the paper on the sander's drum, so drive all nail heads below the surface.

Filling gaps between floorboards

Gaps between boards may bother some more than others. However, you will end up with a more attractive floor, as well as improved draughtproofing, if you make the effort to fill the gaps or close them up.

Closing up

Over a large area, the quickest and most satisfactory solution is to lift the boards a few at a time and re-lay them butted side by side, filling in the final gap with a new board.

Filling with papier mâché

If there are only a few gaps, make up a stiff papier-mâché paste with white newsprint and wallpaper paste, plus a little water-based wood dye to colour the paste to match the sanded floor. Scrape out dirt and wax from between the boards, and press the paste into the gap with a filling knife. Press it well below the level likely to be reached by the sander and fill flush with the floor surface, smoothing the exposed surface with the filling knife.

Inserting a wooden lath

Large gaps can be filled with a thin wooden lath planed to fit tightly between the boards. Apply a little PVA adhesive to the gap and tap the lath in place with a hammer until the wood is flush with the surface. If necessary, skim with a plane. Don't bother to fill several gaps this way: it is easier to close up the boards and fill one larger gap with a new floorboard.

Choosing a sander

The area of a floor is far too large to contemplate sanding with anything but industrial sanding machines. You can obtain the equipment from the usual tool-hire outlets, which will also supply the abrasive papers. You will need three grades of paper: coarse, to level the boards initially, followed by medium and fine to achieve a smooth finish.

It is best to hire a large upright drum sander for the main floor area, and a smaller disc sander for tackling the edges. You can sand smaller rooms, such as bathrooms and WCs, using the edging sander only.

Hire an upright orbital sander for finishing parquet and other delicate flooring that would be ruined by drum sanding.

Some companies also supply a scraper for cleaning out inaccessible corners. If so, make sure it is fitted with a new blade when you hire it.

Hire an upright drum sander for floors.

Using sanding machines

A great deal of dust is produced by sanding a floor, so before you begin, empty the room of furniture and take down curtains, lampshades and pictures. Sweep the floor to remove grit and other debris. Stuff folded newspaper under the door, and seal around it with masking tape. Open all the windows.

In a drum sander, tighten the bar to secure to paper.

Fitting abrasive paper to sanders

Precise instructions for fitting abrasive paper to sanding machines should be supplied with a hired kit. If they are not included, ask the hirer to demonstrate what you need to do. Never attempt to change abrasive papers while a machine is plugged into a socket.

With most drum sanders, the paper is wrapped round the drum then secured in place with a screw-down bar (top left). Ensure that the paper is wrapped tightly around the drum: if it is slack, it may slip from its clamp and will be torn to pieces.

Edging sanders take a disc of abrasive, usually clamped to the sole plate by a central nut (bottom left).

Operating a drum sander

At the beginning of a run, stand with the drum sander tilted back so that the drum itself is clear of the floor. Drape the electrical flex over one shoulder to make sure it cannot become caught in the sander.

Switch on the machine, then gently lower the drum onto the floor. There is no need to push a drum sander: it will move forward under its own power. Hold the machine in check, so that it

Clamp an abrasive disk to an edging sander.

proceeds at a slow but steady walking pace along a straight line. Don't hold it still for even a brief period, or it will rapidly sand a deep hollow in the floorboards. Take care you don't let go of it, either, as it will run across the room on its own, probably damaging the floorboards in the process.

When you reach the other side of the room, tilt the machine back, switch off, and wait for it to stop before lowering it to the floor.

If the abrasive paper rips, tilt the machine onto its back castors and switch off. Wait for the drum to stop revolving, disconnect the power, then change the paper.

Using an edging sander

Hold the handles on top of the machine and drape the flex over your shoulder. Tilt the sander onto its back castors to lift the disc off the floor. Switch on and lower the machine. As soon as you contact the boards, sweep the machine in any direction, but keep it moving – as soon as it comes to rest, the disc will score deep, scorched swirl marks in the wood, which are difficult to remove. There's no need to press down on the machine. When you have finished, tilt back the machine and switch off, leaving the motor to run down.

Hire an edge sander for the areas next to the skirting boards.

Sanding the floor

Old floorboards will most likely be 'cupped' (curved across their width), so the first task is to level the floor across its entire area. With coarse paper fitted to the drum sander, sand diagonally across the room. At the end of the run, tilt the machine, pull it back, and make a second run parallel to the first. Allow each pass to overlap the last slightly. When you have covered the floor once, sweep up the sawdust.

Now sand the floor again in the same way – but this time across the opposite diagonal of the room. Switch off and sweep the dust from the floor.

Change the sanding paper

Once the floor is flat and clean all over, change to a medium-grade paper and sand parallel to the boards. Overlap each pass as before. Finally, switch to the fine-grade paper in order to remove all obvious scratches, working parallel to the boards and overlapping each pass again. Each time you change the grade of paper on the drum sander, put the same grade on the edging sander and sand the edges of the room so that they are finished to the same standard as the main area.

Even the edging sander cannot clean right up to the skirting or into the corners. Finish these small areas with a scraper, or fit a flexible abrasive disc in a power drill.

Vacuum the floor, and wipe it over with a cloth dampened with white spirit ready for finishing.

**After sanding, wipe
the floor with a
dampened cloth
before varnishing.**

Levelling a wooden floor

Tiles, sheet vinyl or carpet should not be laid directly onto an uneven suspended timber floor; the undulations would cause the tiles or covering to lift or even crack. You must create an even, level surface made from hardboard or plywood.

Preparing timber floors

Before you seal the floor with plywood or hardboard, make sure the underfloor ventilation is efficient. Ventilation is extremely important for ground level suspended floors, particularly when floorboards are covered over. Bear in mind, too, that once the floor is sealed you will not have ready access to underfloor pipework and electric cables, so make sure these are in good order.

If you intend to lay hard flooring over floorboards, you'll need thicker board than for soft flooring, otherwise movement in the boards could flip the soft covering off.

Fix down any loose or raised floorboards.

Check loose boards

First of all, check the existing floor for any loose or damaged floorboards. When fixing loose boards over which you intend to lay a sub-floor, it's safer and more accurate to first pilot-drill and then screw them down. Use a vacuum cleaner in all the nooks and crannies, then fix down any loose floorboards firmly.

It is important to match the moisture content of the board and the humidity of the room, or the board will buckle after it has been laid. Soak sheets of hardboard with warm water and leave the sheets stacked back-to-back in the room for 24 hours.

Soak hardboard thoroughly and fix it to the floor while still wet.

①

②

Fixing a plywood sub-floor

The best method for fixing any sub-floor is to temporarily remove any fixtures, such as the toilet and washbasin, before fixing. Alternatively, make a cardboard template of the fittings, transfer this to the plywood and simply cut out the shapes using a jigsaw or a handsaw. Use full-size 2,400 x 1,200mm (8 x 4ft) sheets of plywood where possible. Start by positioning a sheet along the longest wall, then mark the sheet in a grid fashion at 300mm (12in) spacings (1). Pilot-drill and countersink holes at these points, so the screws are fixed level with or just below the plywood surface (2).

Repeat this process until the floorboards are covered, staggering the sheets so that the joints do not align – this is called 'splitting the joints' (3). If the skirting boards are still in place, leave a 3mm (⅛in) gap all around the sub-floor as an expansion gap. If the skirtings have been removed, leave an expansion gap of 10mm (⅜in) all around between the plywood and walls; this gap will be completely concealed when the skirtings are re-positioned.

③

Finally, apply a coat of diluted PVA adhesive to the plywood sub-floor with a paintbrush or roller (4) before laying flooring tiles. This acts as a sealer and bonding agent for the adhesive, simultaneously protecting the plywood sub-floor and improving the degree of adhesion between it and the flooring tiles.

Laying a base for ceramic tiles

A concrete platform is the most suitable base for ceramic floor tiles, but you can lay them on a suspended wooden floor provided the joists are perfectly rigid, so the floor cannot flex. The space below must be adequately ventilated with air bricks, to prevent rot. Level the floor using 15mm (⅝in) marine plywood, screwed down to the joists at 300mm (1ft) intervals. This will create a rigid and flat surface for tiling, less susceptible to expansion and contraction than a boarded floor. Ensure that any joints between sections of board are butted tightly and that there are no proud edges.

Painted and varnished woodwork

Most of the joinery in and around your house will have been painted or varnished at some time; and provided it is in good condition, it will form a sound base for new paintwork.

Stripping down

However, when too many coats of paint have been applied, the mouldings around doorframes and window frames begin to look poorly defined and the paintwork has a lumpy and unattractive appearance. In these cases, it is best to strip off all the old paint down to bare wood and start again. Stripping is also essential where the paintwork has deteriorated and is blistering, crazing or flaking.

Preparing sound paintwork

Wash the paintwork, from the bottom upwards, with a solution of warm water and sugar soap or detergent. Pay particular attention to the areas around the door handles and window catches, where dirt and grease will be heaviest. Rinse with fresh water – from bottom to top, to prevent runs of dirty liquid staining the surface.

Rub down gloss paintwork with fine-grade wet-and-dry abrasive paper, dipped in water, in order to provide a key for the new finish coat and to remove any blemishes.

Prime any bare patches of wood, building up these low spots gradually with undercoat and rubbing down between each application.

Fill open joints or holes with a flexible filler and rub down when set. Renew crumbling putty, and

Dry, flaky paintwork on an outside door.

seal around window frames and doorframes with flexible acrylic filler or mastic, before applying the undercoat and top coat.

Badly weathered paint or varnish

Unsound paintwork or varnish, such as the examples pictured in this section, must be stripped to bare wood. There are several methods you can use, but always scrape off loose material first.

In some cases, where the paint is particularly dry and flaky, dry scraping may be all that is required, using a proprietary hook scraper and finishing with a light rub down with abrasive paper. Where most of the paint is stuck firmly to the woodwork, remove it using one of the methods described on the following pages.

Badly weathered varnish.

Stripping with a blowtorch

The traditional method for stripping old paint is to burn it off with a blowtorch fuelled with liquid gas from a pressurized canister, but you can obtain more sophisticated blowtorches that are connected by a hose to a metal gas bottle of the type used for camping or in caravans. This type of gas torch is finely adjustable, so is also useful for jobs such as brazing and soldering.

Precautions

To reduce the risk of fire, take down curtains and pelmets; outside, rake out old birds' nests from behind your roof fascia board and soffit. Never burn off old (pre-1960s) paint that you suspect may contain lead.

It is only necessary to soften the paint with the flame in order to scrape it off – but it is all too easy to heat the paint so that it is actually burning. Deposit scrapings in a metal paint kettle or bucket as you remove them.

Start by stripping mouldings from the bottom upwards. Never direct the flame at one spot, but keep it moving all the time so that you don't scorch the wood. As soon as the paint has softened, use a shavehook to scrape it off. If it is sticky or hard, heat it a little more and try scraping again.

Having dealt with the mouldings, strip flat areas of woodwork, using a wide-bladed stripping knife. When you have finished stripping, sand the wood with

Strip mouldings with a shavehook.

Heavily overpainted woodwork.

medium-grade abrasive paper to remove hardened specks of paint and any accidental light scorching.

You may find it impossible to sand away heavy scorching without removing too much wood. Sand or scrape off loose blackened wood fibres, then fill any hollows and repaint the woodwork, having primed the scorched areas with an aluminium wood primer.

Using chemical strippers

An old finish can be removed using a stripper that reacts chemically with paint or varnish. There are general-purpose strippers that will soften both solvent- and water-based finishes, including emulsions and cellulose paints, as well as strippers that are formulated to react with a specific type of finish, such as varnish or textured paint. Dedicated strippers achieve the desired result more efficiently than general-purpose ones, but you would have to acquire a whole range of specialist products.

Use a scraper with a blow torch to strip flat surfaces.

Health and safety guidelines

Traditionally, strippers have been made from highly potent chemicals that have to be handled with care. Working with this type of stripper means having to wear protective gloves and safety glasses, and possibly a respirator, too. The newer generation of so-called 'green' strippers do not burn your skin, nor do they exude harmful fumes. However, removing paint with these milder strippers is a relatively slow process.

Whichever type of stripper you use, always follow the manufacturer's health-and-safety guidelines; and if in doubt, err on the side of caution.

Before you opt for a particular stripper, you should also consider the nature of the surface you intend to

must know

Industrial stripping
Any portable woodwork can be taken to a professional stripper, who will immerse the whole thing in a tank of hot caustic-soda stripping solution that must then be washed out of the wood by hosing down with water. It is an efficient process (which incidentally kills woodworm at the same time), but it risks splitting panels, warping the wood and opening up joints. At best, you can expect a reasonable amount of raised grain, which you will have to sand before refinishing.

strip. The thick gel-like paint removers that will cling to vertical surfaces, such as doors and wall panelling, are perfect for all general household joinery. Strippers manufactured to a thinner consistency are perhaps best employed on delicately carved work. For good-quality furniture, especially if it is veneered, make sure you use a stripper that can be washed off with white spirit, as water will raise the grain and may soften old glue.

Working with chemical strippers

Lay polythene sheets or plenty of newspaper on the floor, then apply a liberal coat of stripper to the paintwork, stippling it well into any mouldings. Leave it for 10 to 15 minutes, then try scraping a patch to see if the paint has softened through to the wood. (You might have to leave one of the milder strippers in contact with the paint for 45 minutes or longer.) Don't waste your time removing the top coats of paint only, but apply more stripper and stipple the partially softened finish back down with a brush, so the stripper will soak through to the wood. Leave it for another 5 to 10 minutes.

Once the chemicals have completed their work, use a scraper to remove the softened paint from flat surfaces, and a shavehook to scrape it from mouldings. Wipe the paint from deep carvings with fine wire wool – but when stripping oak, use a nylon-fibre pad impregnated with abrasive material, since oak can be stained by particles of steel wool.

Having removed the bulk of the paint, clean off residual patches with a wad of wire wool – or, in the case of oak, a nylon pad – dipped in fresh stripper. Rub with the grain, turning the wad inside out to present a clean face as it becomes clogged with paint.

Neutralize the stripper by washing the wood with white spirit or water, depending on the manufacturer's recommendations. Let the wood dry out thoroughly, then prepare it the same way as new timber.

Hot-air strippers

Electrically heated guns do the work almost as quickly as a blowtorch, but with less risk of scorching or fire. They operate at an extremely high temperature: never test the stripper by holding your hand over the nozzle. Some guns come with variable heat settings and a selection of nozzles for various uses.

Using a hot-air stripper

Hold the gun about 50mm (2in) from the surface of the paintwork, and move it slowly backwards and forwards until the paint blisters and bubbles. Remove the paint immediately, using a scraper or shavehook. Aim to heat the paint just ahead of either tool, so you develop a continuous work action.

Fit a shaped nozzle onto the gun when stripping glazing bars, in order to deflect the jet of hot air and reduce the risk of cracking the glass.

Old primer is sometimes difficult to remove with a hot-air stripper. This is not a problem if you are repainting the timber: just rub the surface down with abrasive paper. For a clear finish, remove residues of paint from the grain with wads of wire wool dipped in chemical stripper (see *Working with chemical strippers*).

There is less risk of scorching with a hot-air gun.

Treating iron and steel

Metals that are exposed to the elements, or are in close proximity to water, are usually prone to corrosion. Many paints on their own do not afford sufficient protection against corrosion, so special treatments and coatings are often required to prolong the life of the metal.

Remove heavy rust deposits from pitted metal using a wire brush.

What is rust?

Rust is a form of corrosion that affects ferrous metals, notably iron and steel. Although most paints slow down the penetration rate of moisture, they do not keep it out altogether, so a good-quality primer is needed for better protection. The type depends on the condition of the metal and how you plan to decorate it. Make your preparation thorough, or the job could be ruined.

Treating bare metal

Remove light deposits of rust by rubbing with wire wool or wet-and-dry abrasive paper, dipping them in white spirit. If the rust is heavy and the surface of the metal pitted, use a wire brush or, for extensive corrosion, a wire wheel or cup brush in a power drill. Wear goggles to protect your eyes from flying particles.

Use a zinc-phosphate primer to protect metal inside the house. You can use the same primer outdoors, too, but if you are painting previously rusted metal, especially if it is in an exposed location, you will need to use a high-performance rust-inhibitive primer. Work primers into crevices and fixings, and make sure sharp edges and corners are coated generously.

Previously painted metal

If the paint is perfectly sound, wash it with sugar soap or with a detergent solution, then rinse and dry it. Rub down gloss paint with fine wet-and-dry abrasive paper to provide a key.

If the paint film is blistered or is flaking, remove all loose paint and rust with a wire brush or with a wire wheel or cup brush in a power drill. Apply rust-inhibitive primer to any bare patches, working it well into joints, bolt heads and other fixings. Prime bare metal immediately, as rust can re-form very rapidly.

When preparing cast-iron guttering, brush out dead leaves and other debris, then wash it clean. Coat the inside with a bitumen paint. If you want to paint over old bitumen paint, use an aluminium primer first, to prevent it bleeding to the surface.

Stripping painted metal

Delicately moulded sections – on fire surrounds, garden furniture and other cast or wrought ironwork – will often benefit from stripping off old paint and rust masking fine detail. They cannot easily be rubbed down with a wire brush; and a hot-air stripper won't do the job, as the metal would dissipate the heat too quickly for the paint to soften.

Chemical stripping is the safest method, but before you begin, check that the metal fire surround is not in fact made from plaster mouldings on a wooden background. Tap the surround to see if it's metallic or scrape an inconspicuous section.

Paint the bare metal with a rust-inhibitive primer or, alternatively, with a proprietary rust-killing jelly or liquid that will remove and neutralize rust. Usually based on phosphoric acid, these combine with the rust to leave it quite inert, in the form of iron phosphate. Some rust killers will deal with minute particles invisible to the naked eye and are self-priming, so that there is no need to apply an additional primer.

Alternatively, if the metalwork is portable, you may want to take it to a sandblaster or to an industrial stripper. None of the disadvantages of industrial stripping apply to metal. Clean the stripped metal with a wire brush, then wash it with white spirit before applying a finish.

A corroded cast-iron drainpipe.

Cast-iron railings that are deeply pitted with rust.

A rusty casement window sheds its paint.

Preparing tiled surfaces

Used for cladding walls, floors and ceilings, tiles are made in a variety of materials, ranging from ceramic to cork, vinyl and polystyrene, and in different surface textures and finishes. If they become shabby, it's possible to either revive their existing finish or decorate them with paint or wallcoverings.

Make any plaster repairs before tiling.

Paint diluted PVA adhesive on to an old wall to seal the surface.

Work on the walls

Before you even begin tiling, you need to assess the walls and ensure they are sound and as smooth as possible. Any ancient strips of wallcovering or flaky paint and plaster needs to be scraped back. Even if the wall has a smooth painted or plaster surface, sand over it with an electric sander, for better adhesion. Use a two-coat system – undercoat (bonding) and finish plaster – to make any repairs in the plaster. It may be that the wall needs to be completely replastered. In this case, the perfect surface for tiling would be a sand-and-cement plaster, with a wooden or plastic float finish.

Brush on a coat of diluted PVA adhesive once the wall surface has been properly prepared. This seals the surface and aids adhesion when tiling.

Ceramic wall and floor tiles

Ceramic tiles are stuck to the wall or floor with a special adhesive or, in some cases, with mortar. Removing them in their entirety in order to redecorate the wall is messy and time-consuming, but it is often the most satisfactory solution.

Provided a ceramic-tiled wall is sound, you can paint it with a special-purpose primer and compatible gloss paint. Wash the surface thoroughly with sugar-soap or detergent solution, then apply the primer with a synthetic brush. Leave it to harden in a dry steam-free environment for a full 16 hours, then use a natural-bristle brush to apply the gloss.

You can lay new tiles directly over old ones, but make sure the surface is perfectly flat – check by holding a long spirit level or straightedge across the surface. Tap the tiles to locate any loose ones and either glue them firmly in place or chop them out with a cold chisel and club hammer, then fill the space with mortar. Wash the wall to remove grease and dirt.

It is also possible to tile over old quarry or ceramic floor tiles in the same way. Treat an uneven floor with a self-levelling compound.

It is not practicable to paper over old ceramic wall tiles, as the adhesive cannot grip on the shiny surface.

must know

Removing
ceramic tiles
To remove old tiles, chop out at least one of them with a cold chisel, then prise the others off by driving a bolster chisel behind them. Chop away any remaining tile adhesive or mortar with the bolster. Wear goggles to protect your eyes.

Remove a damaged ceramic tile by chopping it away with a cold chisel.

Polystyrene ceiling tiles

You will find that old polystyrene tiles are stuck directly onto the surface with an adhesive that is often difficult to remove. In the past, adhesive was commonly applied in five small dabs – a method that is no longer approved due to the risk of fire. Nowadays, tile manufacturers normally recommend that a complete bed of non-flammable adhesive be used.

Remove old tiles by prising them off with a wide-bladed scraper, and then prise off the dabs of adhesive. Try to soften stubborn patches of adhesive with warm water or wallpaper stripper, wearing goggles and PVC gloves, since it's difficult to avoid splashes.

One way to give old ceiling tiles a face-lift is to paint them – but never be tempted to use a solvent-based paint, as it would increase the risk of fire spreading across the tiles. Instead, brush the tiles to remove dust, and then apply emulsion paint.

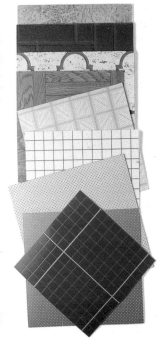

Vinyl floor tiles

To take up vinyl floor tiles, soften the tiles and their adhesive with a thermostatically controlled hot-air gun on a low setting, and use a scraper to prise them up. Remove traces of old adhesive by applying a solution of half a cup of household ammonia and a drop of liquid detergent stirred into a bucket of cold water. When the floor is clean, rinse it with water.

If vinyl tiles are firmly glued to the floor, you can change the colour with a flexible special-purpose vinyl paint. The floor must be cleaned scrupulously, and any silicone-based polish removed with a suitable cleaner. Apply a coat of paint, using a high-density foam roller. Let it dry for four hours, then apply another coat. You can walk on the floor six to eight hours later.

Cork wall tiles

Dense prefinished cork wall tiles can be painted directly, provided that they are clean and firmly attached to the wall.

Prime very absorbent cork with a general-purpose primer first or, when using emulsion or water-based acrylic paint, thin the first coat to reduce absorption.

Unless the tiles are textured or pierced, they can be papered over, but size the surface with commercial size or heavy-duty wallpaper paste, and then apply lining paper to prevent joins showing through.

Cleaning an old quarry-tile floor

Old quarry tiles are absorbent, so the floor becomes ingrained with dirt and grease. If normal washing with detergent fails to revitalize their colour and finish, try one of the industrial preparations available to cleaning companies. Suppliers of industrial tile-cleaning materials are listed in the telephone directory. Describe the type and condition of the tiles to the supplier, who will be able to suggest the appropriate cleaner. Loosen stubborn patches by scrubbing with a plastic scouring pad.

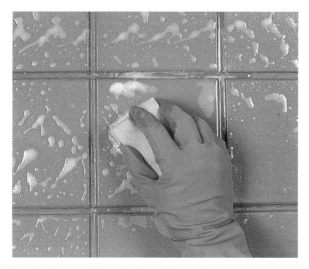

Scrub stubborn patches of grime with a plastic scourer.

want to know more?

Take it to the next level...

▶ **Types of paint** 70–7
▶ **Painting exterior masonry** 79–81
▶ **Applying paint** 87–91
▶ **Painting woodwork techniques** 95–6
▶ **Applying textured coatings** 179

Other sources...
▶ **Join in with a community painting project to practise your skills before unleashing them on your own property.**
▶ **Pick up specialist DIY job preparation leaflets from your local DIY store; all the big chains now offer these for free.**
▶ **Find an internet chat room where you can discuss the best methods for painting and decorating preparation with like-minded souls. A good starting-point is www.diychatroom.com**
▶ **For a wide range of quick and handy tips on general preparation for painting and decorating, consult Collins' *Handy DIY* and *Handy Home Tips*, both available from any good bookshop.**

to
glo
lor
▶
no
jel
up
▶
st
cc
cc

P.
If
a|
be
re
m
c.
a
tl
s
n

(
T
t
e
h
(
I
I
(

3 Paint and painting

There is a bewildering array of different paints on the market today, all of them designed for ever more specific tasks. However, a careful inspection of your local DIY store's paint shelves will reassure you that the choices you make need not actually be that difficult. When it comes to applying the paint, adherence to a few hard and fast rules and following some tried and tested techniques will ensure satisfactory results every time. This chapter tells you everything you really need to know about paint and the skills of painting.

Paint systems

Unless you are using one of the specially formulated one-coat finishes, it is necessary to apply successive layers to build up a paint system.

▶ Painting walls requires a simple system, comprising two or three coats of the same paint.
▶ Painting woodwork and metalwork usually involves a more complex system, using paints with different qualities. A typical paint system for woodwork is illustrated on the left.

A paint system for woodwork

Different types of paint are required to build a protective system for woodwork.
1 Bare timber Sand timber smooth and seal resinous knots with knotting.
2 Primer A primer seals the timber and forms a base for other coats of paint.
3 Undercoat One or two coats obliterate the colour of the primer and build a body of paint.
4 Top coat The final finish provides a wipe-clean coloured surface.

Paint types

▶ **Primer** The first coat of paint applied to provide adequate adhesion between the surface and subsequent topcoats, preventing them sinking into the surface. Can be used on bare wood, plaster or metal. Match a specific primer to the surface.

▶ **Undercoat** A coating applied before the finishing or top coats of a paint job. It may be the first of two or the second of three coats and gives a hard-wearing matt finish.

▶ **Primer undercoat** A combination of primer and undercoat for bare wood surfaces. A quicker alternative to separate primer and undercoat.

▶ **Matt emulsion** A water-based paint giving a flat finish, with little or no sheen. Often used on bare plaster, applying a diluted first coat before the full-strength finishing coat(s).

▶ **Vinyl, silk, satin and eggshell emulsion** These emulsions can be applied on primed or previously painted surfaces, over lining paper or textured wallcoverings. The various choices depend on the degree of 'glossiness' or sheen. Wipeable finish.

▶ **Gloss** This is an oil-based paint which is hard-wearing and easy to clean. Gives a smooth and shiny appearance.

▶ **Textured paint** This is applied on rough-looking plaster to provide a patterned surface. Gives a surface texture to flat walls.

▶ **Floor paint** Formulated to withstand hard wear. They are especially suitable for concrete garage or workshop floors, but they are also used for stone paving, steps and other concrete structures. They can be used inside for playroom floors.

Walls and furniture need specific types of paint.

▶ **Eggshell** An interior mid-sheen oil-based top coat that has a silk-like appearance. Its gloss level is between matt and satin. Unlike gloss, it doesn't reflect imperfections.

Paints for exterior masonry

There are various grades of paint suitable for decorating and protecting exterior masonry, which take into account economy, standard of finish, durability and coverage.

Cement paint

Cement paint is supplied as a dry powder, to which water is added. It is based on white cement, but pigments are added to produce a range of colours. Cement paint is one of the cheaper paints suitable for exterior use. Spray new or porous surfaces with water, then apply two coats.

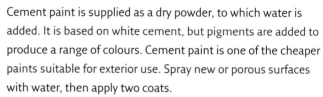

To mix, shake or roll the container to loosen the powder, then add 2 volumes of powder to 1 of water in a clean bucket. Stir it to a smooth paste, then add a little more water until you achieve a full-bodied creamy consistency. Mix no more than you can use in one hour, or it will start to dry.

▶ **Adding an aggregate** When you're painting a dense wall, or one treated with a stabilizing solution so its porosity is reduced, it is advisable to add clean sand to the mix to give it body. This also provides added protection for an exposed wall and helps to cover dark colours. If the sand changes the colour of the paint, add it to the first coat only. Use 1 part sand to 4 parts powder, stirring it in when the paint is still in its paste-like consistency.

Masonry paints

When buying weather-resistant exterior-masonry paints, you have a choice between a smooth matt finish or a fine granular texture.

▶ **Water-based masonry paint** Most masonry paints are water-based, being in effect exterior-grade emulsions with additives that prevent mould growth. Although they are

It's a good idea to wear protective gloves with exterior paints.

supplied ready for use, on porous walls it pays to thin the first coat with 20 per cent water – then follow up with one or two full-strength coats, depending on the colour of the paint.

Water-based masonry paints must be applied during fairly good weather. Damp or humid conditions and low temperatures may prevent the paint drying properly.

▶ **Solvent-based masonry paints** Some masonry paints are thinned with white spirit or with a special solvent – but unlike most oil paints they are moisture-vapour permeable, so that the wall is able to breathe. It is often advisable to thin the first coat with 15 per cent white spirit, but check the manufacturer's recommendations.

Solvent-based paints can be applied in practically any weather conditions, provided it is not actually raining.

▶ **Reinforced masonry paint** Masonry paint that has powdered mica or a similar fine aggregate added to it dries with a textured finish that is extremely weatherproof. Reinforced masonry paints are especially suitable in coastal districts and in industrial areas – where dark colours are also an advantage, in that dirt will not show up as clearly as on a pale background. Although large cracks and holes must be filled prior to painting, reinforced masonry paint will cover hairline cracks and crazing.

Textured coating

A thick textured coating can be applied to exterior walls to form a thoroughly weatherproof self-coloured coating, which can be overpainted to match other colours. The usual preparation is necessary, and brickwork needs to be pointed flush. Large cracks should be filled, although a textured coating will cover fine cracks. The paste is either brushed or rolled onto the wall, then left to harden, forming an even texture. However, if you prefer, you can produce a texture of your choice, using a variety of simple tools. It's a relatively easy process, but practise on a small section first.

Paints for interior surfaces

Emulsion paint is most people's first choice for internal decorations: it is relatively cheap and practically odourless, and there are several qualities of paint to suit different circumstances. However, some situations demand a combination of paints to provide the required degree of protection or simply to achieve a pleasing contrast of surface textures.

Vinyl emulsions are the most popular and practical paints for walls and ceilings. They are available in liquid or thixotropic consistencies, with matt or satin (semi-gloss) finishes.

A satin emulsion is less likely to show fingerprints or scuffs. Non-drip thixotropic paints have obvious advantages when painting ceilings.

One-coat emulsion

If you are to avoid a patchy, uneven appearance, you need to apply two coats of a standard emulsion paint, perhaps thinning the first coat slightly when decorating porous surfaces. A one-coat high-opacity emulsion is intended to save you time – but you won't get satisfactory results if you try to spread the paint too far, especially when overpainting strong colours.

Emulsion is the obvious choice of paint for walls and ceilings.

New-plaster emulsions

These emulsions are formulated for painting newly plastered interior walls and ceilings, to allow moisture vapour to escape. Standard vinyl emulsions are not sufficiently permeable.

Anti-mould emulsion

This low-odour emulsion contains a fungicide to ward off mould growth. Paints primarily intended for woodwork can also be applied to walls and ceilings that require an extra degree of protection. Similar paints are ideal for decorating the disparate elements of a period-style dado – wooden rail, skirting and embossed wallcovering. Gloss paints tend to accentuate uneven wall surfaces, so most people prefer a satin (eggshell) finish.

You can use any of the standard spirit-thinned paints on walls and ceilings; but if fast drying is a priority, choose a water-based acrylic paint.

Sheen levels

Top coat paints come in different levels of sheen; the level of sheen, or gloss, determines whether the paint absorbs or reflects light. The choice of sheen depends on how the room is being decorated.

▶ **Matt** A flat finish with little sheen.

▶ **Silk or satin vinyl emulsion** Sometimes referred to as eggshell by some manufacturers. More of a sheen; popular choice for kitchens, bathrooms, children's rooms and hallways.

▶ **Satinwood or semi-gloss** This finish falls in between the above levels of sheen.

▶ **Gloss** Leaves a shiny, smooth finish. Rarely used on walls.

Safety when painting

Solvents in paint (volatile organic compounds – VOCs) contribute to atmospheric pollution and can exacerbate conditions such as asthma. Where possible, it's therefore preferable to use paints and varnishes with low VOC emissions. Most manufacturers label their products to indicate the level of VOCs.

must know

Disposing of unwanted paint
Before you wash your brushes and rollers, wipe them on newspaper to remove as much paint as possible. Ask your local authority about facilities for disposing of waste paint and cans.

Take precautions

Take sensible precautions when using solvent-based paints:

▶ Ensure good ventilation indoors while applying a finish and when it is drying. Wear a respirator if you suffer from breathing disorders.
▶ Don't smoke while painting or in the vicinity of drying paint.
▶ Contain paint spillages outside with sand or earth, and don't allow any paint to enter a drain.
▶ If you splash paint in your eyes, flush them with copious amounts of water, with your lids held open. If symptoms persist, visit a doctor.
▶ Always wear barrier cream or gloves if you have sensitive skin. Use a proprietary skin cleanser to remove paint from your skin, or wash it off with warm soapy water. Don't use paint thinners to clean your skin.
▶ Keep all finishes and thinners out of reach of children. If a child swallows a substance, don't make any attempt to induce him or her to vomit – seek medical treatment, instead.

Painting exterior masonry

The outside walls of houses are painted for two main reasons: to give a bright, clean appearance, and to protect the surface from the weather. What you use as a finish and how you apply it depends on what the walls are made from, their condition and the degree of protection they need.

Exterior walls

Bricks are traditionally left bare, but may require a coat of paint if previous attempts to decorate have resulted in a poor finish. Rendered walls are often painted to brighten the naturally dull grey colour of the cement; pebbledashed surfaces may need a colourful coat to disguise unsightly patches. Or you may, of course, simply want to change the present colour of your walls for a fresh appearance.

Painting a house can be daunting, so divide the job into manageable sections.

Working to a plan

Before you embark upon painting the outside walls of your house, plan your time carefully. Depending on the amount of preparation that is required, even a small house will take a few weeks to complete.

Use the chart on the opposite page to help you work out approximately how much time to allow a particular finish to dry, how many coats a surface might need and roughly how much of a certain finish you need.

It's not necessary to tackle the whole job at once, although it is preferable, since the weather may change to the detriment of your timetable. You can split the work into separate stages with days (or even weeks) in between, provided you divide the walls into manageable sections. Use window frames and doorframes, bays, downpipes and corners of walls to form break lines that will disguise joins.

Start at the top of the house – working from right to left, if you are right-handed.

must know

Painting concrete floors, steps or structures
The floor or other concrete area must be clean, dry and free from oil or grease. If the concrete is freshly laid, allow it to mature for at least a month before painting. In most cases it is advisable to prime powdery or porous floors with a proprietary concrete sealer, but check manufacturers' recommendations first. The best way to paint a large area is to use a paintbrush around the edges, then fit an extension to a paint roller for the bulk of the floor or concrete structure.

Finishes for masonry

	Cement paint	Water-based masonry paint	Reinforced masonry paint	Solvent-based masonry paint	Textured coating	Floor paint
SUITABLE TO COVER						
Brick	•	•	•	•	•	•
Stone	•	•	•	•	•	•
Concrete	•	•	•	•	•	•
Cement rendering	•	•	•	•	•	•
Pebbledash	•	•	•	•	•	•
Emulsion paint		•	•	•	•	•
Solvent-based paint		•	•	•	•	•
Cement paint	•	•	•	•	•	•
DRYING TIME: HOURS						
Touch-dry	1-2	1-2	2-3	4-6	6	2-3
Recoatable	24	4-6	24	16	24-48	3-16
THINNERS: SOLVENTS						
Water	•	•	•		•	•
White spirit			•	•		•
NUMBER OF COATS						
Normal conditions	2	2	1-2	2	1	1-2
COVERAGE: DEPENDING ON WALL TEXTURE						
Sq metres per litre		4-10	3-6.5	6-16	2	5-10
Sq metres per kg	1-6				1-2	
METHOD OF APPLICATION						
Brush	•	•	•	•	•	•
Roller	•	•	•	•	•	•
Spray gun	•	•	•	•		

• Black dot denotes compatibility. All surfaces must be clean, sound, dry and free from organic growth

Masonry painting techniques

Once you have chosen the type of exterior finish, you then have to decide on which is the best method of applying that particular medium. In most cases the choice is down to which technique is the quickest and most efficient for the task.

Using paintbrushes

Choose a brush 100 to 150mm (4 to 6in) wide for painting walls; larger ones are heavy and tiring to use. A good-quality brush with coarse bristles will last longer on rough walls. For effective coverage, apply the paint with vertical strokes, crisscrossed with horizontal ones. You will need to stipple paint into textured surfaces.

Protect downpipes with newspaper.

Cutting in

Painting up to a doorframe or window frame is known as cutting in. It's tricky to paint a reasonably straight edge following the line of the feature on a heavily textured wall. Don't just apply more paint; instead, touch the tip of the brush only to the wall, using a gentle scrubbing action, then brush out from the edge to spread excess paint once the texture is filled.

Painting behind pipes

To protect rainwater downpipes, tape a roll of newspaper around them. Stipple behind the pipe with a brush, then slide the paper tube down the pipe to mask the next section.

Painting with a banister brush

Use a banister brush for pebbledash.

Use a banister brush to paint deep textures such as pebbledash. Pour paint into a roller tray and dip the brush in to load the bristles. Scrub the paint onto the wall, using circular strokes to work it into the uneven surface.

Using a paint roller

A roller will apply paint three times faster than a brush. Use a long-pile roller for heavy textures, and one with a medium pile for lightly textured or smooth walls. Rollers wear out very quickly on rough walls, so have a spare sleeve handy in these situations. When painting with a roller, vary the angle of the stroke to ensure even coverage; use a brush to cut into awkward angles and any obstructions.

Use the correct roller for the texture.

Using a spray gun

Spraying is the quickest and most efficient way to apply paint to a large expanse of wall, but you will have to mask all the parts you don't want to paint, using newspaper and masking tape, and erect plastic screening to prevent overspray.

Thin the paint by about 10 per cent; and set the spray gun according to the manufacturer's instructions, to suit the particular paint. It's advisable to wear a respirator.

Hold the gun about 225mm (9in) away from the wall and keep it moving with even, parallel passes. Slightly overlap each pass and try to keep the gun pointing directly at the surface. Trigger the gun just before each pass, and release it at the end of the stroke.

To cover a large blank wall evenly, spray it with vertical bands of paint, overlapping each band by 100mm (4in).

Painting interior walls & ceilings

Unless your house is newly built, most of the interior walls and ceilings will be plastered, and probably papered or painted, too. Preparation varies, but the methods for painting them are identical. A matt paint is usually preferred, but there's no reason why you shouldn't use a gloss or satin finish.

Extra brushes such as (above, left to right) a radiator brush and a cutting-in brush can be useful.

Paints for walls and ceilings

Emulsion paint, in its many forms, is the most practical finish for interior surfaces, but you can use an acrylic or solvent-based paint on wall-fixed joinery such as skirtings, architraves and picture rails.

Textured paints

Provided the masonry or plaster is sound, you can cover any unsightly cracks with one coat of textured paint. A coarse high-build paint will cover cracks up to 2mm (⅟₁₆in) wide. There are also fine-texture paints for areas where people are likely to brush against a wall. Available in either a matt or satin finish, the paint is normally applied with a coarse-foam roller.

Cement paint

This inexpensive exterior finish is also ideal for a utilitarian area indoors such as a cellar, garage or workshop. Sold in dry-powder form, it has to be made up with water and dries to a matt finish.

Paintbrushes

Apart from the standard kit of brushes, which will have widths of 25, 50, 75 and 100 or 125mm (1, 2, 3, 4 or 5in), you may decide to add a couple of extra brushes to your collection. A cutting-in brush has bristles cut at an angle for painting window frames without smudging the glass. This type of brush comes in widths of 12, 18 and 25mm (½, ¾ and 1in). A radiator brush has a long handle for reaching down behind radiators, so they don't have to be taken off the wall. A paint kettle allows you to decant large tins of paint.

The best quality paintbrushes are made of natural animal bristle and will last a long time if looked after well. However, you get what you pay for and these brushes are usually the most expensive to buy. Cheaper brushes made from synthetic fibres are readily available and some are getting almost to the quality of the natural bristle brushes. The bristles of the most expensive synthetic brushes are made from polyester and nylon, and produce a better finish than cheaper types. On the whole, synthetic fibre brushes are really only best used for rough work and undercoating.

watch out!

Cover up
Take time to carefully cover any floor finishes with dust sheets and always decant large tins of paint into smaller containers in case of any accidental spills.

Paint rollers

You can apply paint more quickly using a paint roller than you can do with a brush – and another major advantage is that they are less tiring to use. Rollers are generally used with emulsion paint to cover large areas such as walls and ceilings.

Paint rollers cover large areas such as walls and ceilings much faster than using a brush.

Rollers come in a variety of sleeve materials to suit specific jobs: foam for general-purpose work; mohair for a smooth finish; shag pile for textured or roughcast surfaces. Rollers are generally sold together with a tray into which to pour the paint. Simply load the roller by running it backwards and forwards in the paint. The disadvantages of rollers are that they tend to use a lot of paint, rarely give a truly smooth surface finish and you will still need a brush for corners and cutting-in work.

Ceilings before walls

Always paint the ceiling first, to avoid splashing the walls or paintwork. Remove any splashes immediately with a damp sponge or cloth. If the ceiling is to be a different colour to the walls, paint the ceiling and be sure to overlap the paint onto the walls.

When painting the walls, carefully cut the paint into the ceiling angle rather than the other way around. Cut in the awkward areas first, such as the skirting or the ceiling edges, with a paintbrush. Then paint the rest with a roller. For a superior finish, always use two coats, even if the instructions on the paint tin say otherwise. Between each coat of paint, rub down with a very fine sandpaper, called flour paper, as this will remove any dust that may have settled before the paint dried.

Finishes for bare masonry

Interior walls may be left unplastered for the sake of appearance or because it is unnecessary to clad the walls of rooms such as a basement, workshop or garage. A brick or stone chimney breast can be an attractive focal point, while an entire wall of bare masonry may make a dramatic impression.

If you want to finish brick, concrete or stone walls, follow the methods for exterior walls. However, because in this case they do not have to withstand any weathering, you can use paints designed for interiors.

Rub down with flour paper between coats.

Take extra care when painting up to skirting boards.

Applying paint

Erect a work platform, placing it so that you can cover as much of the surface as possible without changing position: you will achieve a better finish and will be able to work in safety.

Applying paint by brush

Choose a good-quality brush for painting walls and ceilings. Cheap brushes tend to shed bristles – which is annoying and also less economical in the long run. A brush about 200mm (8in) wide will allow you to cover a surface relatively quickly, but if you are not used to handling a large brush your wrist will soon tire. You may find a 150mm (6in) brush, plus a 50mm (2in) brush for the edges and corners, more comfortable to use. However, the job will take longer.

Loading the brush

Don't overload a brush with paint; it leads to messy work, and ruins the bristles if the paint is allowed to dry in the roots. Dip no more than the first third of the brush into the paint, wiping off excess on the inside of the container to prevent drips. When using thixotropic paint, load the brush and apply paint without removing excess.

Using a brush

You can hold the brush whichever way feels comfortable to you, but the 'pen' grip is the most versatile, enabling your wrist to move the brush freely in any direction. Hold the brush handle between your thumb and forefinger, with your

Having brushes of various widths can help cover most paint jobs.

fingers on the ferrule (metal band) and your thumb supporting it from the other side.

Apply the paint in vertical strokes, then spread it at right angles to even out the coverage. Finish oil paints with light upward vertical strokes, to avoid leaving brushmarks in the finished surface. This technique – known as laying off – is not necessary when applying emulsion paint.

Applying paint by roller

A paint roller with interchangeable sleeves is an excellent tool for applying paint to large areas and is quicker than using a brush. Choose a roller about 225mm (9in) long for painting walls and ceilings. Larger ones are available, but they become tiring to use after a time.

There are a number of different sleeves to suit the type of paint and texture of the surface. Long-haired sheepskin and synthetic-fibre sleeves are excellent on textured surfaces, especially when applying emulsion paint. Choose a shorter pile for smooth surfaces, and when using gloss or satin paints. Disposable plastic-foam rollers can be used to apply some specialist paints, but they soon lose their resilience and have a tendency to skid across the wall.

Special rollers

Rollers with long detachable extension handles are ideal for painting ceilings without having to erect work platforms.

Narrow rollers for painting behind radiators are invaluable if the radiators cannot be removed from the wall.

Loading a roller

You will need a special paint tray to load a standard roller. Pour the paint into the paint tray. Having dipped the sleeve lightly into the paint reservoir, roll it gently onto the ribbed part of the tray to coat the roller evenly.

Using a roller

Use random, zigzag strokes with a roller, painting the surface in all directions to achieve even coverage. Keep the roller on the surface at all times – if you let it spin at the end of a stroke, it will spatter paint onto the floor or adjacent surfaces. When applying any type of solvent-based paint, finish in one direction, preferably towards prevailing light.

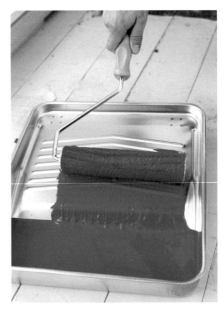

Load the roller by running it backwards and forwards in the paint tray.

Applying paint by pad

Paint pads for large surfaces have flat rectangular faces covered with a short mohair pile. A plastic-foam backing gives the pad flexibility, so that the pile will always be in contact with the wall, even on a rough surface.

The exact size of the pad will be determined by the brand you choose, but one about 200mm (8in) long is best for applying paint evenly and smoothly to walls and ceilings. You will also need a small pad or paintbrush for cutting in at corners and ceilings.

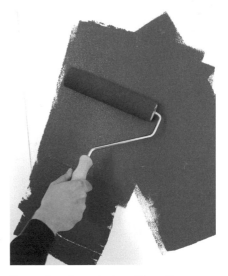

Use random zigzag strokes with a roller.

Loading a pad

Load a pad from its own special tray, drawing the pad across the captive roller so that you pick up an even amount of paint.

Using a paint pad

To apply the paint consistently, keep the pad flat on the wall and sweep it gently and evenly in any direction. However, to prevent streaking, finish with vertical strokes when using solvent-based paints.

Painting techniques

The way you apply your paint is vital – never overload your brush. Before painting walls with either a brush or a roller, go around with a narrow brush to cover the edges, the corners and the space around light switches, etc., where a roller or larger brush won't reach without smudging. Paint one wall at a time so that you can complete the wall before the margins dry, otherwise you will be left with a hard line showing through. Use brushes and rollers in random directions when applying emulsion.

Techniques such as painting the edges (above, top) and covering the corners (above) with a narrow brush can achieve impressive end results (right).

Finishes for interior walls & ceilings

	Emulsion	One-coat emulsion	New-plaster emulsion	Solvent-based paint	Acrylic paint	Textured paint	Cement paint
SUITABLE TO COVER							
Plaster	•	•	•	•	•	•	•
Wallpaper	•	•	•	•	•		
Brick	•	•	•	•	•	•	•
Stone	•	•	•	•	•	•	•
Concrete	•	•	•	•	•	•	•
Previously painted surface	•	•	•	•	•	•	
DRYING TIME: HOURS							
Touch-dry	1-2	3-4	1-2	2-4	1-2	24	1-2
Recoatable	4		4	16-18	4		24
THINNERS: SOLVENTS							
Water	•	•	•		•	•	•
White spirit				•			
NUMBER OF COATS							
Normal conditions	2	1		1-2	1-2	1	2
COVERAGE: DEPENDING ON WALL TEXTURE							
Sq metres per litre	9-15	8	11	15-16	10-14	2-3	
Sq metres per kg							1-6
METHOD OF APPLICATION							
Brush	•	•	•	•	•	•	•
Roller	•	•	•	•	•	•	•
Spray gun	•	•	•	•	•		

• Black dot denotes compatibility. All surfaces must be clean, sound, dry and free from organic growth

Finishing woodwork

Paint is the most common finish for woodwork in and around the house, offering as it does a protective coating in a choice of colours and surface finishes.

Wipe over woodwork before painting to remove any dust.

Painting woodwork

Before you even begin painting, wash down woodwork with sugar soap, then, using a damp cloth, wipe it over to remove any dust. For a really impressive finish, apply two coats of undercoat before painting with a finish coat of an oil-based paint.

Not just paint

However, stains, varnishes, lacquers and polishes give an attractive, durable finish to joinery, enhancing the colour of the woodwork without obliterating the beauty of its grain. When choosing a finish, bear in mind the location of the woodwork and the amount of wear it is likely to get.

Choosing wood finishes

The next two pages detail a range of finishes for protecting and decorating woodwork. Each can be suitable for a particular purpose, although many can be employed simply for their attractive appearance rather than for any practical considerations.

Solvent-based paints

Traditional solvent-based paints (oil paints) are available in high-gloss and satin finishes, with both liquid and thixotropic consistencies. Indoors, they will last for years, with only the occasional wash-down to remove fingermarks. One or two undercoats are essential, especially outside, where durability is considerably reduced by the action of sun and rain.

Acrylic paints

These have several advantages over conventional oil paint. Being water-based, they are non-flammable, practically odourless, and constitute less of a risk to health and to the environment. They also dry quickly, so that a job can often be completed in a day. However, this means you have to work swiftly when decorating outside in direct sunlight, to avoid leaving brushmarks.

Wood dyes

Unlike paint, which after the initial priming coat rests on the surface of timber, a dye penetrates the wood. Its main advantage is to enhance the natural colour of the woodwork or to unify the slight variation in colour found in even the same species.

Protective wood stains

The natural colour of wood can be enhanced with protective wood stains. Being moisture-vapour permeable, they allow the wood to breathe while providing a weather-resistant satin finish

must know

Varnishes
Exterior-grade varnishes are more weather-resistant; and some of them, including yacht varnish, are tough enough to cope with polluted urban environments and coastal climates.

that resists flaking and peeling. Opaque colours are also available.

Coloured preservers

Sawn-timber fencing, wall cladding and outbuildings tend to look particularly unattractive when painted, yet they need protection. Use a wood preserver, which penetrates deeply into the timber to prevent rot and insect attack. There are clear preservers, plus a range of natural-wood colours.

Varnishes

Varnish is a clear protective coating for timber. Most modern varnishes are made with polyurethane resins to provide a waterproof, scratchproof and heat-resistant finish. They come in high-gloss, satin or matt finishes.

Cold-cure lacquer

This plastic coating is mixed with a hardener just before it is used. It is extremely durable (even on floors) and is resistant to heat and alcohol. The standard type dries to a high gloss, which can be burnished to a lacquer-like finish if required.

Finishing oil

Oil is a subtle finish that soaks into the wood, leaving a mellow sheen on the surface. Traditional linseed oil remains sticky for hours, whereas a modern oil will dry in about an hour and provides a tougher, more durable finish.

Wax polishes

Wax can be employed to preserve and maintain another finish or as a finish itself. A good wax should be a blend of beeswax and a hard polishing wax such as carnauba. Some contain silicones to make it easier to achieve a high gloss. Although very attractive, it is not a durable finish and should be used indoors only.

must know

Wood stains
Protective wood stains are invariably brushed onto the wood. Some wood-stain manufacturers recommend two to three coats, while others offer a one-coat finish. Some ranges include a clear finish for redecorating previously stained woodwork without darkening the existing colour. Water-based stains generally tend to dry faster than those thinned with a spirit solvent.

Painting woodwork

Wood is a fibrous material with a definite grain pattern and different rates of absorption. And some species contain knots that may ooze resin. These are all qualities that have a bearing on the type of paint you use when decorating as well as the techniques and tools you need to apply it.

Basic application

It is essential to prepare and prime all new woodwork thoroughly before applying the finishing coats.

If you're going to use conventional solvent-based paint, apply one or two undercoats, depending on the covering power of the paint. As each coat hardens, rub down with fine wet-and-dry paper to remove blemishes, then wipe the surface with a cloth dampened with white spirit.

Apply the paint with vertical brush-strokes, and then spread it sideways to even out the coverage. Finish with light strokes ('laying off') in the direction of the grain. Blend the edges of the next application while the paint is still wet. Don't go back over a painted surface that has started to dry, or you will leave brushmarks in the paintwork.

Use a different technique for spreading one-coat or acrylic paints. Simply lay on the paint liberally with almost parallel strokes, then lay off lightly. Blend wet edges quickly.

Best-quality paintbrushes are the most efficient tools for painting woodwork. You will need 25 and 50mm (1 and 2in) brushes for general work, and a 12mm (½in) brush for painting narrow glazing bars.

To finish an area with a straight edge, use one of the smaller brushes and place it a few millimetres from the edge. As you flex the bristles, they will spread to the required width, laying on an even coat of paint.

Finishes for woodwork

	Solvent-based paint	Acrylic paint	Wood dye	Protective wood stain	Coloured preserver	Varnish	Acrylic varnish	Cold-cure lacquer	Oil	Wax polish	French polish
SUITABLE TO COVER											
Softwoods	•	•	•	•	•	•	•	•	•	•	
Hardwoods	•	•	•	•	•	•	•	•	•	•	•
Oily hardwoods	•	•	•	•		•	•	•	•	•	•
Planed wood	•	•	•	•	•	•	•	•	•	•	•
Sawn wood					•						
Interior use	•	•	•	•		•	•	•	•	•	•
Exterior use	•	•		•	•	•	•		•		
DRYING TIME: HOURS											
Touch-dry	4	1-2	0.5	0.5-4	1-2	2-4	0.5	1	1		0.5
Recoatable	16	4-6	6	4-16	2-4	14	2	2	6	1	24
THINNERS: SOLVENTS											
Water		•	•	•	•		•				
White spirit	•		•	•	•	•			•	•	
Methylated spirit											•
Special thinner								•			
NUMBER OF COATS											
Interior use	1-2	1-2	2-3	1-2		2-3	3	2-3	3	2	10-15
Exterior use	2-3	1-2		1-2	2	3-4	3-4		3		
COVERAGE: DEPENDING ON WALL TEXTURE											
Sq metres per litre	15-16	10-14	16-30	10-25	4-12	15-16	15-17	16-17	10-15	Variable	Variable
METHOD OF APPLICATION											
Brush	•	•	•	•	•	•	•	•	•	•	•
Paint pad	•	•	•	•		•	•	•			
Cloth pad (rubber)			•			•	•		•	•	•
Spray gun	•	•		•	•	•	•	•			

• Black dot denotes compatibility. All surfaces must be clean, sound, dry and free from organic growth

Painting doors

Doors have a variety of faces and conflicting grain patterns, all of which need to be painted separately – yet the end result must look even in colour, with no ugly brushmarks or heavily painted edges. There are certain procedures for painting all types of door.

Preparation and technique

Remove the door handles and wedge the door open so that it cannot be closed accidentally, locking you inside the room. Keep the handle in the room with you, just in case.

Aim to paint the door and frame separately, so there's less chance of touching wet paintwork when passing through a freshly painted doorway. Paint the door first; then when it's dry, finish the framework.

If you want to use a different colour for each side of the door, paint the hinged edge the colour of the closing face (the one that comes to rest against the frame). Paint the outer edge of the door the same colour as the opening face – so there won't be any difference in colour when the door is viewed from either side.

Each side of the frame should match the corresponding face of the door. Paint the frame in the room into which the door swings – including the edge of the stop bead against which the door closes – to match the opening face. Paint the rest of the frame the colour of the closing face.

System for a flush door

To paint a flush door, start at the top and work down in sections, blending each one into the other. Lay on

Paint the mouldings first with a panelled door.

the paint, then finish each section with light vertical strokes. Finally, paint the edges, taking extra care to avoid paint runs.

System for a panelled door

The different parts of a panelled door must be painted in a logical sequence. Finish each part with strokes running parallel to the direction of the grain.

Whatever style of panelled door you are painting, start with the mouldings followed by the panels. Paint the muntins (centre verticals) next and then the cross rails. Finish the face by painting the stiles – the outer verticals. Last of all, paint the edge of the door.

To achieve a superior finish, paint the muntins, rails and stiles together, picking up the wet edges of the paint before they begin to dry. Take care not to overload the brush when using gloss paint.

must know

Removing specks and bristles
Don't attempt to remove brush bristles or specks of fluff from fresh paintwork once a skin has started to form. Instead, let the paint harden, then rub down with wet-and-dry paper. The same applies if you discover runs.

Apply paint by 'laying off' across the grain.

Painting window frames

Like doors, window frames need to be painted in sequence so that the various components will be coated evenly – and also so you can close the windows at night. Clean the glass thoroughly before painting a window.

Painting a casement window

A casement window hinges like a door, so if you plan to paint each side a different colour, follow a similar procedure to that recommended for painting doors and frames.

It's best to remove the stay and catch before you paint the window – but so that you can still operate the window without touching wet paint, drive a nail into the underside of the bottom rail and use it as a makeshift handle.

Painting sequence

First paint the glazing bars, cutting into the glass on both sides. Carry on with the top and bottom horizontal rails, followed by the vertical stiles. Finish the casement by painting the edges; then paint the frame.

Painting a sash window

The following sequence describes the painting of a sash window from the inside. To paint the outside face, use a similar procedure – but start with the lower sash. If you are using different colours for each side, the demarcation lines are fairly obvious: when the window is shut, all the visible surfaces from one side should be the same.

The bristles of a cutting-in brush are cut at an angle to help you work right up to the glass.

A plastic or metal shield enables you to paint a straight edge right up to glass.

Painting sequence

Raise the bottom sash and pull down the top one. Paint the bottom meeting rail of the top sash and the accessible parts of the vertical members. Reverse the position of the sashes, leaving a gap top and bottom, and complete the painting of the top sash. Paint the bottom sash, and then the frame except for the runners in which the sashes slide.

Leave the paint to dry, then paint the inner runners plus a short section of the outer runners, pulling the cords aside to avoid brushing paint on them, as this will make them brittle and shorten their working lives. Before the paint has time to dry, check that the sashes slide freely.

Protecting the glass

When painting the sides of wooden glazing bars, overlap the glass by about 2mm (⅟₁₆in) to prevent rain or condensation seeping between the glass and woodwork.

If you find it difficult to achieve a satisfactory straight edge, use a proprietary plastic or metal paint shield, holding it against the edge of the frame, to protect the glass.

Alternatively, run masking tape around the edges of the windowpane, leaving a just a slight gap so that the paint will seal the join between glass and frame. When the paint is touch-dry, carefully peel off the tape. Don't wait until the paint is completely dry or the film of paint may peel off with the tape.

Scrape the glass with a sharp blade to remove any dry paint spatters. Many DIY stores sell plastic handles to hold blades for this purpose.

must know

UPVC paint and restorer
To clean ingrained dirt from UPVC windows and doors, use a proprietary surface-restorer on a damp cloth. If that doesn't revive the colour, you can redecorate badly weathered UPVC windows and doors with a special fast-drying gloss paint.

Finishing metalwork

Ferrous metals that are rusty will shed practically any paint film, so the most important aspect of finishing metalwork is thorough preparation and priming, to prevent the corrosion from returning. Applying the finish is virtually the same as for woodwork.

Methods of application

With the exception of black lead, you can use a paintbrush to apply metal finishes. In general, the techniques are identical to those used for painting woodwork, but don't attempt to brush out bitumen-based paints in the conventional manner.

Remove metal door and window fittings for painting, suspending them on wire hooks to dry. Make sure that sharp edges are coated properly, as the finish can wear thin relatively quickly.

Some paints can be sprayed, but there are few situations where this is advantageous, except perhaps in the case of intricately moulded ironwork such as garden furniture, which you can paint outside. Indoors, good ventilation is essential.

A roller is suitable for large flat surfaces. Pipework requires a special V-section roller, designed to coat curved surfaces.

Radiators and pipes

Leave radiators and hot-water pipes to cool before you paint them. The main problem with a radiator is how to paint the back: the best solution is to remove it completely or use a special radiator roller or brush with a long handle (see top page 102).

Paint pipework lengthwise rather than across, or runs are likely to form. The first coat on metal piping will be streaky, so be prepared to apply two or three coats. Allow the paint to harden thoroughly before turning on the heat.

must know

Bitumen-based paints
Bitumen-based paints give economical protection for exterior storage tanks and piping. Standard bituminous paint is black, but there is also a limited range of colours, plus 'modified' bituminous paint, which contains aluminium.

3 Paint and painting

A long slim-handled radiator brush or roller enables you to paint the back of a radiator without having to remove it from the wall.

Finishes for metalwork

	Solvent-based paint	Hammered-finish paint	Metallic paint	Bitumen-based paint	Security paint	Radiator enamel	Black lead	Lacquer	Bath paint	Non-slip paint
DRYING TIME: HOURS										
Touch-dry	4	0.5	4	1–2		0.5		0.25	6–10	4–6
Recoatable	14	1–3	8	6–24		4			16–24	12
THINNERS: SOLVENTS										
Water					•	•				
White spirit	•		•	•			•		•	•
Special		•								
Cellulose thinners								•		
NUMBER OF COATS										
Normal conditions	1–2	1	1–2	1–3	1	2	Variable	1	2	2
COVERAGE: DEPENDING ON WALL TEXTURE										
Sq metres per litre	12–16	3–5	10–14	6–15	2.5	15	Variable	18	13–14	3–5
METHOD OF APPLICATION										
Brush	•	•	•	•	•	•	•	•	•	•
Paint pad	•	•		•						
Spray gun	•	•		•				•		
Cloth pad (rubber)							•			

• Black dot denotes compatibility. All surfaces must be clean, sound, dry and free from organic growth

Suitable finishes for metalwork

▶ **Solvent-based paints** Once it has been primed, interior metalwork will need at least one undercoat, plus a top coat. Add an extra undercoat to protect exterior metalwork.

▶ **Hammered-finish paint** This is a combination of heat-hardened glass flakes, aluminium particles and resins, and is applied as one coat only, even on previously rusted metal.

▶ **Metallic paints** Choose a paint containing aluminium, copper, gold or bronze powder. They can withstand temperatures up to about 100°C (212°F) and are water-resistant.

▶ **Security paints** Non-setting security paint, primarily for rainwater and waste downpipes, remains slippery to prevent intruders from scaling the wall via the pipe.

▶ **Radiator enamels** Fast-drying water-based radiator enamel is supplied in a variety of colours, including satin chrome. Radiator enamel can be applied to previously painted radiators, provided the surfaces are thoroughly cleaned and lightly sanded. Bare metal radiators must be coated with a compatible primer.

▶ **Black lead** A cream used for cast ironwork, black lead is a mixture of graphite and waxes. It is reasonably moisture-resistant, but is not suitable for exterior use.

▶ **Lacquer** Clear lacquer can be used on polished metalwork without spoiling its appearance. To protect chrome plating, brass and copper, use a clear acrylic metal lacquer.

▶ **Non-slip paints** Designed to provide secure footholding on a wide range of surfaces, including metal, non-slip paints are ideal for metal staircase treads and exterior fire escapes. The surface must be primed before application.

want to know more?

Take it to the next level...

▶ **Colour schemes** 19-21
▶ **Painted and varnished woodwork** 54-9
▶ **Preparing iron and steel** 60-61
▶ **Changing trends** 170
▶ **Other paint effects** 176

Other sources...
▶ **Learn more about exterior paints and techniques for decorating outdoors at www.sandtex.co.uk**
▶ **For ideas about which paints to use and how to use them to create personalized colour schemes, try one of the many interior design magazines available on the market.**
▶ **Rent a painting and decorating video from your local library or buy one at most DIY stores. These are now widely available.**
▶ **Check out the excellent website at www.paintquality.co.uk for a wide range of up-to-date information on all aspects of paint and painting, including this season's most popular decorating trends.**

4 Wallpapering

Wallpapers have been used for hundreds of years. They offer a number of useful advantages over paint in that they will cover a multitude of sins on old or badly rendered walls and offer considerable variety if you fancy some sort of pattern or motif as well as colour on the walls of your living space. However, applying wallpaper is not one of the easier disciplines in decorating; it can take quite a lot of practice in order to become proficient at the various techniques involved. The following pages explain the basics of how to proceed whilst offering numerous useful tips.

Wallcoverings

Although wallcoverings are often called 'wallpaper', only a proportion of the wide range available is made solely from wood pulp. There is a huge range of paper-backed fabrics, from exotic silks to coarse hessians.

1 Hand-printed
2 Machine-printed

Choice in coverings

Other types include natural textures such as cork or woven grass on a paper backing. Plastics have widened the choice of wallcoverings still further: there are paper-backed or cotton-backed vinyls, and plain or patterned foamed plastics. Before wallpaper became popular, fabric wall hangings were used to decorate interiors; and this is still done today, using unbacked fabrics glued or stretched across walls.

Ensuring a suitable surface

Although many wallcoverings will cover minor blemishes, walls and ceilings should be clean, sound and smooth. Eradicate damp and organic growth before hanging any wallcovering.

Coverings that camouflage

Although a poor surface should be repaired, some coverings hide minor blemishes, as well as providing a foundation for other finishes.

Expanded-polystyrene sheet

A thin polystyrene sheet is used for lining a wall before papering. It reduces condensation and also bridges hairline cracks and small holes. Polystyrene dents easily, so don't use it where it will take a lot of punishment. There is a patterned version for ceilings.

Lining paper

This is a cheap buff-coloured wallpaper for lining uneven or
impervious walls prior to hanging a heavy or expensive
wallcovering. It also provides an even surface for emulsion paint.

Woodchip paper

Woodchip paper is made by sandwiching particles of wood
between two layers of paper. It is inexpensive, easy to hang (but
a problem to cut), and must be painted.

Types of wallcovering

Printed wallpapers

One advantage of ordinary wallpaper is the superb range of
printed colours and patterns, which is much wider than for
any other wallcovering. Most of the cheaper papers are
machine-printed.

The more costly hand-printed papers are prone to tearing
when wet, and inks have a tendency to run if you smear paste
on the surface. They are not really suitable for walls exposed to
wear or condensation. Pattern matching can be awkward,
because hand printing isn't as accurate as machine printing.

Relief papers

Wallpapers that have deeply embossed patterns hide minor
imperfections. Reliefs are invariably painted, with emulsion,
satin-finish oil paints or water-based acrylics.

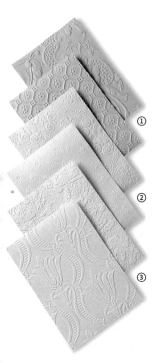

1 Lincrusta
2 Embossed-paper
wallcovering
3 Blown vinyl

Lincrusta, which was the first embossed wallcovering, consists of a solid film of linseed oil and fillers fused onto a backing paper before the pattern is applied with an engraved steel roller. It is still available, though many people prefer embossed-paper wallcoverings or the superior-quality versions made from cotton fibres. Lightweight vinyl reliefs are also popular.

Washable papers

These are printed papers with a thin impervious glaze of PVA to make a spongeable surface. Washables are suitable for bathrooms and kitchens. The surface must not be scrubbed, or the plastic coating will be worn away.

Vinyl wallcoverings

A base paper, or sometimes a cotton backing, is coated with a layer of vinyl upon which the design is printed. Heat is used to fuse the colours and vinyl. The result is a durable, washable wallcovering ideally suited to bathrooms and kitchens. Many vinyls are sold ready-pasted for easy application.

Foamed-plastic covering

This is a lightweight wallcovering made solely of foamed polyethylene with no backing paper. It is printed with a wide range of patterns, colours and designs. You paste the wall instead of the covering.

Flock wallcoverings

Flock papers have the major pattern elements picked out with a fine pile produced by gluing synthetic or natural fibres (such as silk or wool) to the backing paper; the pattern stands out in relief, with a velvet-like texture. Standard flock papers are difficult to hang, as contact with paste will ruin the pile. Vinyl flocks are less delicate, can be hung anywhere, and may even come ready-pasted.

Grass cloth

Natural grasses are woven into a mat and glued to a paper backing. While these wallcoverings are very attractive, they are fragile and difficult to hang.

Cork-faced paper

This is surfaced with thin sheets of coloured or natural cork. It is not as easily spoiled as other special papers.

Paper-backed fabrics

Finely woven cotton, linen or silk on a paper backing has to be applied to a flat surface. They are expensive and not easy to hang, so avoid smearing the fabric with adhesive.

Unbacked fabrics

Upholstery-width fabric – typically hessian – can be wrapped around panels, which are then glued or pinned to the wall.

1 Washable papers
2 Textured and patterned vinyl
3 Foamed polyethylene
4 Flock papers
5 Paper-backed fabric
6 Grass-cloth mats
7 Cork-faced paper

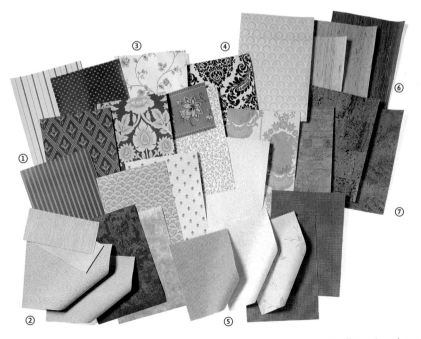

Wallcoverings: quantities

Calculating the number of rolls of wallcovering you need will depend mainly on the size of the roll. However, you also need to take into consideration the pattern repeat and to make allowance for cutting around obstructions such as windows and doors.

You will need all these tools for wallpapering.

Size of rolls

The width of a standard roll of wallcovering is 520mm (1ft 9in), the length 10.05m (33ft). Use the charts in this section to estimate how many rolls you need for walls and ceilings.

Calculate the amount you need the following way:

Walls

Measure the height of the walls from skirting to ceiling. Divide the length of the roll by this figure to find the number of wall lengths you can cut from a roll. Measure around the room to determine how many widths fit into the total length of the walls.

Ceilings

Measure the room length to determine one strip of paper. Work out how many roll-widths fit across the room.

Measure the perimeter of the ceiling.

Ceilings: Number of (standard) rolls required

Measurement around room	Number of rolls	Measurement around room	Number of rolls	Measurement around room	Number of rolls	Measurement around room	Number of rolls
11m	2	16m	4	21m	6	26m	9
12m	2	17m	4	22m	7	27m	10
13m	3	18m	5	23m	7	28m	10
14m	3	19m	5	24m	8	29m	11
15m	4	20m	5	25m	8	30m	11

Height of room in metres from skirting

Look down the height column and across the wall column to estimate the number of standard rolls required.

WALLS (m)	2–2.25m	2.25–2.5m	2.5–2.75m	2.75–3m	3–3.25m	3.25–3.5m	3.5–3.75m	3.75–4m
	NUMBER OF (STANDARD) ROLLS REQUIRED FOR WALLS							
10	5	5	6	6	7	7	8	8
10.5	5	6	6	7	7	8	8	9
11	5	6	7	7	8	8	9	9
11.5	6	6	7	7	8	8	9	9
12	6	6	7	8	8	9	9	10
12.5	6	7	7	8	9	9	10	10
13	6	7	8	8	9	10	10	10
13.5	7	7	8	9	9	10	10	11
14	7	7	8	9	10	10	11	11
14.5	7	8	8	9	10	10	11	12
15	7	8	9	9	10	11	12	12
15.5	7	8	9	9	10	11	12	13
16	8	8	9	10	11	11	12	13
16.5	8	9	9	10	11	12	13	13
17	8	9	10	10	11	12	13	14
17.5	8	9	10	11	12	13	14	14
18	9	9	10	11	12	13	14	15
18.5	9	10	11	12	12	13	14	15
19	9	10	11	12	13	14	15	16
19.5	9	10	11	12	13	14	15	16
20	9	10	11	12	13	14	15	16
20.5	10	11	12	13	14	15	16	17
21	10	11	12	13	14	15	16	17
21.5	10	11	12	13	14	15	17	18
22	10	11	13	14	15	16	17	18
22.5	11	12	13	14	15	16	17	18
23	11	12	13	14	15	17	18	19
23.5	11	12	13	15	16	17	18	19
24	11	12	14	15	16	17	18	20
24.5	11	13	14	15	16	18	19	20
25	12	13	14	15	17	18	19	20
25.5	12	13	14	16	17	18	20	21
26	12	13	15	16	17	19	20	21
26.5	12	14	15	16	18	19	20	22
27	13	14	15	17	18	19	21	22
27.5	13	14	16	17	18	20	21	23
28	13	14	16	17	19	20	21	23
28.5	13	15	16	18	19	20	22	23
29	13	15	16	18	19	21	22	24
29.5	14	15	17	18	20	21	23	24
30	14	15	17	18	20	21	23	24

Pasting wallcoverings

You can use any wipe-clean table for pasting, but a narrow fold-up pasting table is a good investment if you are doing a lot of decorating. Lay several cut lengths of paper face down on the table to keep it clean.

Choosing paste

Most wallpaper pastes are supplied as powder or flakes for mixing with water. Some come ready-mixed.

▶ **All-purpose paste** Standard wallpaper paste is suitable for most lightweight to medium-weight papers. With less water added, it can be used to hang heavyweight papers.

▶ **Heavy-duty paste** This is specially prepared for hanging embossed papers, paper-backed fabrics and other heavyweight wallcoverings.

▶ **Fungicidal paste** Pastes often contain a fungicide to prevent mould developing under impervious wallcoverings, such as vinyls, washable papers and foamed-plastic coverings.

▶ **Ready-mixed paste** Tubs of ready-mixed thixotropic paste are specially made for heavyweight wallcoverings and fabrics.

▶ **Stain-free paste** Use with delicate papers that could be stained by conventional pastes.

▶ **Repair adhesive** Sticks down peeling edges and corners. It will glue vinyl to vinyl, so is suitable for applying decorative border rolls.

Applying the paste

Use a large, soft wall brush or pasting brush to apply. Mix the paste in a plastic bucket and tie string across the rim to support the brush, keeping its handle clean while you hang the paper.

Align the wallcovering with the far edge of the table, to avoid brushing paste on the table – where it could be

Cut the wallcovering into measured lengths using wallpaper shears.

transferred to the face of the wallcovering. Apply the paste by brushing
away from the centre. Paste the edges
and remove any lumps.

If you prefer, apply the paste with a
short-pile paint roller. Pour the paste
into a roller tray and roll it onto the
wallcovering in one direction only,
towards the end of the paper.

Pull the wallcovering to the front
edge of the table and paste the other
half. Fold the pasted end over – don't
press it down – and slide the length along the table to
expose an unpasted section.

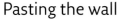

Paste the other end, then fold it over to almost meet the
first cut end. The second fold is invariably deeper than the first –
a handy way to tell which is the bottom of patterned
wallcoverings. Fold long drops concertina-fashion.

Hang vinyls and lightweight papers immediately; drape
other wallcoverings over a broom handle spanning two chair
backs, or other supports, and leave to soak. Some heavy or
embossed wallcoverings need to soak for 15 minutes.

**Apply the paste down
the centre of the
paper, then brush it
away to the sides.**

Pasting the wall
Instead of pasting the back of exotic wallcoverings, paste the
wall, to reduce the risk of marking their delicate faces. Apply a
band of paste just wider than the length of wallcovering, so you
won't have to paste right up to its edge for the next length. Use
a brush or roller.

Ready-pasted wallcoverings
Many wallcoverings come precoated with adhesive, activated by
soaking a cut length in a trough of cold water. Plastic troughs
are sold for the purpose.

must know

**Cutting plain
wallcoverings**
Measure the
height of the wall
at the point where
you will hang the
first 'drop'. Add an
extra 100mm (4in)
for trimming top
and bottom. Cut
several pieces and
mark the top of
each one.

Papering a wall

Don't apply a wallcovering of any kind until all the woodwork in the room has been painted or varnished, and the ceiling painted or papered.

Hold the folded paper in one hand and smooth it onto the wall, starting top right. Butt strips of paper together or leave a slight gap.

Lining a wall

Lining a wall before papering is only necessary if you are hanging embossed or luxury wallcoverings, or if the wall has imperfections that might show through a thin wallpaper.

Mark a horizontal line on the wall one roll-width from the ceiling. Start at the top right-hand corner of the wall, aligning the bottom edge with the marked line. Smooth the paper onto the wall, working from the centre towards the edges of the paper. Work along the wall, unfolding the length as you go. Lightly mark the corner, peel back the paper and trim to the line. Brush the paper back in place. Work down the wall, butting each strip against the last.

Trim the bottom length to the skirting. Leave the lining paper to dry out for 24 hours before covering.

Where to start

The traditional method is to hang the first length next to a window close to a corner, then work in both directions away from the light. But it may be easier to paper the longest uninterrupted wall first to get used to the techniques before tackling corners or obstructions. If your wallcovering has a large regular motif, centre the first length over the fireplace for symmetry, or centre this first length between two windows.

Hanging on a straight wall

The walls of a room are rarely truly square, so use a plumb line to mark a vertical guide against which to hang the first length of wallcovering. Start at one end of the wall and mark the vertical line one roll-width away from the corner minus 12mm (½in), so the first length will overlap the adjacent wall.

Allowing enough wallcovering for trimming at the ceiling, unfold the top section of the pasted length and hold it against the plumbed line. Brush the paper gently onto the wall, working from the centre in all directions in order to squeeze out any trapped air.

When you are sure the paper is positioned accurately, lightly draw the point of your scissors along the ceiling line, peel back the top edge, and cut along the crease. Smooth the paper back and tap it down with the brush. Unpeel the lower fold of the paper, smooth it onto the wall with the brush, then tap it into the corner. Crease the bottom edge against the skirting, peel away the paper, then trim and brush it back against the wall.

Hang the next length in the same manner. Slide it with your fingertips to align the pattern and produce a perfect butt joint. Wipe any paste from the surface with a damp cloth. Continue to the other side of the wall, allowing the last drop to overlap the adjoining wall by 12mm (½in).

Suspend a plumb line from the ceiling.

Use a straight-edge to mark the vertical.

Brush out any trapped air.

Use a seam roller to ensure the join is stuck down properly.

Make sure there is a good crease for cutting.

Corners and obstructions

It is rare to find a straightforward room, with perfect walls and no awkward fixtures and fittings to paper around, so it is wise to know how to cope with these problems before the event.

Interior corners.

Exterior corners.

Cut diagonally from the centre.

Papering around corners

Turn the corner by marking another plumbed line so that the next length of paper covers the overlap from the first wall. If the piece you trimmed off at the corner is wide enough, use it as your first length on the new wall. If there's an alcove on both sides of the fireplace, you will need to wrap the paper around the external corners. Trim the last length so that it wraps around the corner, lapping the next wall by about 25mm (1in).

Papering behind radiators

If you can't remove a radiator, measure the positions of the brackets fixing it to the wall. Transfer the measurements to a length of wallcovering and slit it from the bottom to the top of the bracket. Feed the pasted paper behind the radiator, down both sides of the brackets. Use a radiator roller to press it to the wall.

Papering around switches and sockets

Turn off the electricity supply. Hang the wallcovering over the switch or socket, then make diagonal cuts from the centre of the fitting to each of its corners. Trim off the waste, leaving about 6mm (¼in). Loosen the faceplate, tuck the margin behind, and retighten. Switch the power back on when the paste is dry.

Papering around doors and windows

When you get to the door, hang the length of paper next to a doorframe, brushing down the butt joint to align the pattern and allowing the other edge to loosely overlap the door.

Make a diagonal cut in the excess towards the top corner of the frame. Crease the waste down the side with scissors, peel it back, trim off, then brush back. Leave a 12mm (½in) strip for turning on the top of the frame.

Fill in with short strips above the door, then butt the next full length of paper over the door and cut the excess diagonally into the frame, pasting the rest of the strip down the other side of the door. Mark and cut off the waste.

If a window is set into a reveal, hang the length of wallcovering next to the window and allow it to overhang. Make a horizontal cut above the edge of the reveal. Make a similar cut near the bottom, then fold the paper around to cover the side of the reveal. Crease and trim along the window frame and sill.

Cut the excess overlap around the door diagonally into the frame.

To fill in the window reveal, first cut a strip of wallcovering to match the width and pattern of the overhang above the reveal. Paste it, slip it under the overhang, and fold it around the top of the reveal. Cut through the overlap with a smooth wavy stroke, then remove the excess paper and roll down the joint.

Papering around a fireplace

Papering around a fireplace is similar to a doorframe. Make a diagonal cut in the waste overlapping the fireplace, cutting towards the corner of the mantel shelf. Now tuck the paper in all round for creasing and trimming to the surround.

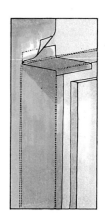

Fold onto reveal top.

If the surround is ornate, brush the paper onto the wall above the surround, then trim the paper to fit under the mantel shelf at each side; brush around the corners of the chimney breast to hold it in place. Gently press the wallcovering into the shape of the fire surround, peel it away, and then cut round the impression with nail scissors. Smooth the paper back down with the brush.

Papering stairwells

The problem when papering a stairwell is having to handle the extra-long drops on the side walls; and for this, you need to build a safe work platform over the stairs.

A safe platform can be either hired scaffold or a combination of stepladders and boards.

Hanging tips

Plumb and hang the longest drop first, lapping the head wall above the stairs by 12mm (½in).

Carrying the long drops of wall-covering – sometimes as much as 4.5m (15ft) long – is awkward. Paste the covering liberally, so it's not likely to dry out while you hang it, then fold it concertina-fashion; drape it over your arm while you climb the platform. You will need an assistant to support the weight of the pasted length while you apply it. Unfold the flaps as you work down the wall.

Pad the tops of ladders to protect a newly decorated wall.

Crease and cut the bottom of the wallcovering against the angled skirting (don't forget to allow for this angle when cutting each piece to length). Work away from this first length in both directions, then paper the head wall.

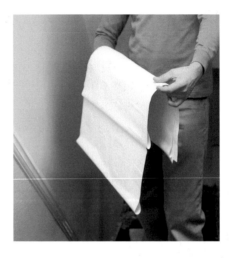

To avoid making difficult cuts, it pays to arrange the strips so that the point at which the banister rail meets the wall falls between two butted joints. Hang the drops to the rail and cut horizontally into the edge of the last strip at the centre of the rail, then make radial cuts so the paper can be tapped in around the rail. Crease the flaps, peel away the wallcovering, and cut them off. Smooth the covering back in place.

For ease, fold paper into a 'concertina' arrangement.

Hang the next drop at the other side of the rail, butting it to the previous piece, and make similar radial cuts.

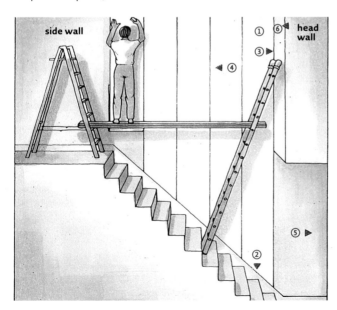

side wall   ① ⑥◀ head wall
③▶
◀④
⑤▶
②▼

Special techniques

No matter what kind of wallcovering you are using, most of the standard wallpapering techniques previously explained hold good. However, there are some additional considerations and special techniques involved in applying some types of wallcovering.

Relief wallcoverings

Line the wall before hanging embossed-paper wallcoverings. Apply a heavy-duty paste liberally and evenly to the wallcovering, but try not to leave too much paste in the depressions. Allow each piece to soak for 10 minutes (15 minutes for cotton-fibre wallcoverings) before you hang it. Don't turn a relief wallcovering around corners. Instead, measure the distance from the last drop to the corner and cut your next length to fit.

Vinyl wallcoverings

Paste paper-backed vinyls in the normal way. Cotton-backed vinyl hangs better if you paste the wall and then leave it to become tacky before you apply the wallcovering. Hang and butt-join lengths of vinyl, using a sponge instead of a brush to smooth them onto the wall.

Ready-pasted wallcoverings

Place the trough of cold water at the bottom of the first drop. Roll a cut length loosely from the outside and immerse the roll in the trough for the prescribed time, according to instructions. Hanging a long wet length can be difficult if you follow the standard procedure. Instead, roll the length from the top with the pattern outermost. Place it in the trough and immediately reroll it through the water. Take it from the trough in roll form and drain off excess water, then unroll the strip as you hang it.

Fabrics and special coverings

Try to keep paste off the face of paper-backed fabrics and other special wallcoverings. To avoid ruining an expensive paper, ask the supplier which paste to use for the wallcovering you have chosen. Many special wallcoverings have delicate surfaces, so use a felt or rubber roller to press the covering in place, or tap gently with a brush.

Pull paper from the trough and hang it on the wall.

Unbacked fabrics

There are two ways to apply unbacked fabric to your walls.

If you want to hang a plain-coloured medium-weight fabric, you can stick it directly onto the wall.

However, it can be difficult to align patterns when the fabric stretches. For more control over a patterned fabric, stretch it onto panels of lightweight insulation board 12mm (½in) thick – which gives you the double advantage of insulation and a pin-board – and attach the boards directly to the wall.

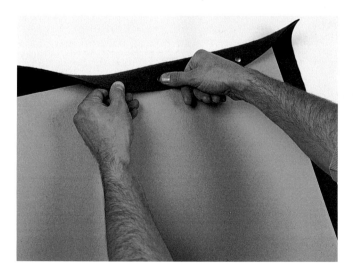

Stretch unbacked fabric over insulation board.

Papering a ceiling

Papering a ceiling isn't as difficult as you may think. The techniques are basically the same as for papering a wall, except that the drops are usually longer and so more unwieldy to hold while brushing the paper into place.

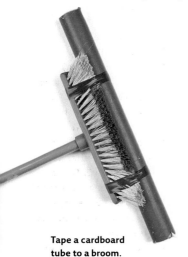

Tape a cardboard tube to a broom.

If you have to work from a stepladder, get someone to support the paper on a home-made support (see tube and broom, above).

Setting out the ceiling

Set up a sensible work platform, as it's virtually impossible to work from a single stepladder. The best type of platform to use is a purpose-made decorator's trestle, but you can manage with a pair of scaffold boards spanning two stepladders. Enlist a helper to support the folded paper while you position one end.

Now mark the ceiling to give a visual guide to positioning the strips of paper. Aim to work parallel with the window wall and away from the light, so you can see what you are doing and so that the light will not highlight the joins between strips. If the distance is shorter the other way, then it's easier to hang the strips in that direction.

Mark a guideline along the ceiling one roll-width minus 12mm (½in) from the side wall, so that the first strip of paper will lap onto the wall.

Putting up the paper

Paste the paper as for a wallcovering and fold it in a concertina arrangement. Drape the folded length over a spare roll and carry it to the work platform. You will find it easier if a helper supports the folded paper, leaving both your hands free for brushing it into place.

Hold the strip against the guideline, using a brush to stroke it onto the ceiling. Tap it into the wall angle, then gradually work backwards along the scaffold board, brushing the paper on as your helper unfolds it.

If the ceiling has a cornice, crease and trim the paper at the ends. Otherwise leave it to lap the walls by 12mm (½in), so that it will be covered by the wallcovering. Work across the ceiling in the same way, butting the lengths of paper together. Cut the final strip roughly to width, and trim to lap onto the wall as before.

Light fittings and centrepieces

Unlike walls, where you have doors, windows and radiators to contend with, there are few obstructions on a ceiling to make papering difficult. However, problems can occur where there is a pendant light fitting or a decorative plaster centrepiece.

Cutting around a pendant light

Where the paper passes over a ceiling rose, cut several triangular flaps so that you can pass the light fitting through the hole. Tap the paper all round the rose with a paperhanger's brush, then continue on to the end of the length. Return to the rose and cut off the flaps with a knife. Remember to switch off the power if you expose the wiring.

Papering around a centrepiece

If you have a decorative centrepiece, work out the position of the strips so that a join will pass through the middle. Cut long flaps from the side of each piece, so you can tuck it in all round. Always take care to obscure the edges of the paper underneath the edge of the centrepiece and glue them firmly to the ceiling.

want to know more?

Take it to the next level...

▶ **Colour schemes** 19-21
▶ **Preparing plasterwork** 36-7
▶ **Patching plasterwork** 38-9
▶ **Preparing wallcoverings** 40-41
▶ **Choosing carpets** 156-9

Other sources...

▶ For excellent up-to-date information on all aspects of wallpapering and wallcoverings in general, check out www.wallpapers-uk.com. This website features sections on latest trends, how to makeover a room, brand new wallpaper styles from top designers and much more.
▶ Try television interior design and room makeover shows for hot tips and contemporary ideas about how to get more from your walls.

5 Tiling walls

Ceramic wall tiles come in all shapes, sizes, colours and designs, offering great variety and a reasonably inexpensive way of personalizing a kitchen, bathroom or other utilitarian living space. Of course, the great advantage of tiles is that they are hardwearing and waterproof, which is why they are most often used in steamy, moist environments. Applying tiles is not as difficult as you might think, and can be extremely rewarding. If you apply your own you will also save a great deal of money, as tiling is regarded as a specialist trade.

Choosing tiles

Tiling allows you to cover a surface with relatively small regular units that can be cut and fitted into awkward shapes far more easily than sheet materials. With an almost inexhaustible range of colours, textures and patterns to choose from, tiling is one of the most popular methods of decorating walls.

Ceramic wall tiles

The majority of ceramic wall tiles are coated with a thick layer of glaze that makes them durable, waterproof and relatively easy to cut. Unglazed tiles are generally more subtle in colour, and may need to be sealed to prevent them absorbing grease and dirt.

Machine-made tiles are perfectly regular in shapes and colour, and are therefore simple to lay

Commercially available ceramic tiles come in virtually every shape, size and colour.

and match. With hand-made tiles, there is much more variation in shape, colour and texture, but this irregularity merely adds to their appeal.

Although rectangular tiles are available, the majority of wall tiles are 100 or 150mm (4 or 6in) square. As well as a wide range of plain colours, you can buy printed and high-relief moulded tiles in both modern and traditional styles. Patterned tiles can be used for decorative friezes or individual inserts; and some are sold as sets for creating pictorial murals, mostly for cooker and basin splashbacks.

Narrow border tiles are used to create visual breaks that relieve the monotony of large areas of regular tiling. You can also buy purpose-made skirting and cornice tiles.

Cross-shape plastic spacers are used to maintain regular gaps between standard field tiles.

Mosaic tiles

These are in effect small versions of the standard ceramic tiles. To lay them individually would be time-consuming and lead to inaccuracy, so they are usually joined, either by a paper covering or a mesh backing, into larger panels. Square tiles are common, but rectangular, hexagonal and round mosaics are also available. Because they are small, mosaics can be used on curved surfaces and fit irregular shapes better than large ceramic tiles do.

Mosaic tiles mostly come in panels (top two examples) but can come in individual shapes.

Above: Polystyrene tiles.

Below: Mineral-fibre tiles.

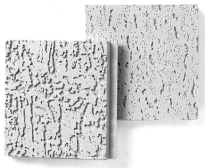

Polystyrene tiles

Although expanded-polystyrene tiles will not significantly reduce heat loss from a room, they are able to prevent condensation and mask a ceiling that is in poor condition. Polystyrene cuts easily, provided the trimming knife is very sharp. For safety in case of fire, choose a self-extinguishing type and do not overpaint with an oil paint. Polystyrene wall tiles are made, but they crush easily and are not suitable for use in a vulnerable area. The tiles may be flat or decoratively embossed.

Mineral-fibre tiles

Ceiling tiles made from compressed mineral fibre are dense enough to be sound-insulating and heat-insulating. They are normally fitted into a suspended grid system that may be exposed or concealed, depending on whether the tile edges are rebated or grooved. Fibre tiles can also be glued directly to a flat ceiling. A range of textured surfaces is available.

Mirror tiles

Square and rectangular mirror tiles are attached to walls by means of a self-adhesive pad in each corner. Both silver and bronze finishes are available. Mirror tiles will present a distorted reflection unless they are mounted on a perfectly flat surface.

Plastic tiles

Insulated plastic wall tiles inhibit condensation. Provided you don't use abrasive cleaners on them, they are relatively durable; but they will melt if subjected to direct heat. A special grout is applied to fill the 'joints' moulded across the 300mm (1ft) square tiles.

Cork tiles

Cork is can also be a covering for walls, as well as floors. It is easy to lay with contact adhesive, and can be cut to size and shape with a knife. A wide choice of textures and warm colours is available. Presanded but unfinished cork will darken in tone when you varnish it. Alternatively, you can buy ready-finished tiles with various plastic and wax coatings.

A selection of mirror tiles (left) and plastic tiles (right).

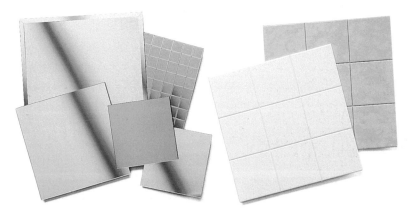

Setting out wall tiles

Having prepared the wall surfaces for tiling, the next stage is to measure each wall accurately, in order to determine where to start tiling and how to avoid having to make too many awkward cuts. The best way is to mark a row of tiles on a straight wooden batten, which you can use as a gauge stick for setting out the walls.

Setting out a plain wall

On an uninterrupted wall, use the gauge stick to plan horizontal rows of tiles, starting at skirting level. If you are left with a narrow strip at the top, move the rows up half a tile-width to create a wider margin. Then mark the bottom of the lowest row of whole tiles.

Temporarily nail a thin guide batten to the wall aligned with the mark. Place a spirit level on top to check it is horizontal.

Mark the centre of the wall, then set out vertical rows on each side of the line with the gauge stick. If the margin tiles measure less than half a width, reposition sideways by half a tile.

must know

Making a gauge stick

Make a gauge stick from 50 x 18mm (2 x ¾in) softwood to help you plot the position of the tiles on the wall. Lay several tiles along the stick, inserting plastic spacers between them, and mark the position of each tile on the softwood batten.

Plotting a half-tiled wall

If you are tiling part of a wall only – up to a dado rail, for example – set out the tiles to leave a row of whole tiles at the top. If you are incorporating skirting tiles or border tiles, plan their positions first and use them as starting points.

Arranging tiles around a window

For nicely balanced tiling, you should always use a window as your starting point, so that the tiles surrounding it are equal in size but not too narrow. If possible, begin a row of whole tiles at sill level and position cut tiles at the back of the window reveal. If necessary, fix a guide batten over a window to support a row of tiles temporarily.

Renovating wall tiles

A properly tiled surface should last for many years, but the appearance is often spoiled by discoloured grouting or cracked tiles. Or perhaps you just want a change of colour. There is usually no need to retile the wall, as these problems can be solved fairly easily.

Painting ceramic wall tiles

You can change the appearance of glazed ceramic tiles with a water-resistant one-coat tile paint. Clean the surfaces thoroughly, and scrub the grout lines with a nailbrush to remove traces of grease or mould growth. Dry the tiles, then apply the paint with a natural-bristle brush. If you want to pick out individual tiles, protect the surrounding tiles with masking tape. You may have to apply a second coat of paint to cover dark colours or heavily patterned tiles.

When the paint is dry, redraw the grout lines with a compatible grout pen. You can use a similar pen to brighten up discoloured grout without having to repaint the tiles.

Renovate old wall tiles with one-coat tile paint.

Replacing a cracked ceramic tile

Scrape the grout from around the damaged tile, then use a small cold chisel to chip out the tile, working from the centre. Wear protective goggles, and take care not to dislodge neighbouring tiles.

Scrape out the remains of the old adhesive, and brush debris from the recess. Butter the back of the replacement tile with adhesive, then press it firmly in place. Wipe any excess from the surface, and allow the adhesive to set before renewing the grout.

Retouch the joints with a grout pen.

Fixing ceramic wall tiles

Start by tiling the main areas with whole tiles, leaving the narrow gaps around the edges to be filled with cut tiles later. This will allow you to work relatively quickly and to check the accuracy of your setting out before you have to make any tricky cuts.

Choosing adhesive and grout

Ceramic tiles are stuck to the wall with special adhesives that are generally sold ready-mixed, although a few need to be mixed to a paste with water. Grout is a similar material that is used to fill the gaps between the tiles.

Most tile adhesives and grouts are water-resistant, but check that any material you use for tiling shower surrounds is completely waterproof. If tiles are to be laid on a wallboard, make sure you use a flexible adhesive. Heat-resistant adhesive and grout may be required in the vicinity of a cooker and around a fireplace. You should use an epoxy-based grout for worktops to keep them germ-free.

Form ridges with a notched spreader.

Applying whole tiles

A serrated plastic spreader is normally supplied with each tub of adhesive, but if you are tiling a relatively large area, buy a larger notched metal trowel. Use the straight edge of the spreader or trowel to spread enough adhesive to cover about 1m (3ft) square; then turn the tool around and drag the notched edge through the adhesive to form horizontal ridges.

Press the first tile into the angle formed by the setting-out battens. Press the next tile into place with a slight twist until it is firmly fixed, using plastic spacers to form the grout lines between the tiles. Lay additional tiles to build up three or four rows at a time, then wipe any adhesive from the surface of the tiles with a clean damp sponge.

Stick the first tile against the setting-out battens.

Spread more adhesive and continue to tile along the batten until the first rows of whole tiles are complete. From time to time, check that your tiling is accurate by holding a batten and spirit level across the faces and along the top and side edges.

When you have completed the entire field, scrape adhesive from the margins and allow the rest to set firm before removing the setting-out battens.

Marking and fitting margin tiles

Cut tiles one at a time to fit the gaps between the field tiles and adjacent walls, because walls are never truly square and the margins are bound to be uneven.

Mark each margin tile by placing it face down over its neighbour with one edge against the adjacent wall; allow for the normal spacing between the tiles. Transfer the marks to the edges of the tile using a felt-tip pen. Having cut it to size (see overleaf), spread adhesive onto the back of each tile and press it into the margin.

Grouting

Standard grouts are white, grey or brown, but there is also a range of coloured grouts to match or contrast with the tiles. Alternatively, mix coloured pigments with dry powdered grout, before adding water.

Leave the tile adhesive to harden for 24 hours, then use a rubber-bladed spreader or a tiler's rubber float to press grout into the joints.

Using a barely damp sponge, wipe grout from the surface before it sets. When the grout has dried, polish the tiles with a dry cloth.

To make sure the grout hardens thoroughly, don't use a newly tiled shower for about seven days.

Mark the back of a margin tile.

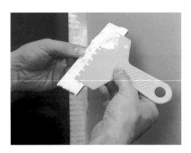

Butter adhesive onto the back of a cut tile.

Press grout into the joints with a rubber spreader.

Cutting ceramic tiles

For any but the simplest projects, you will have to cut tiles to fit around obstructions, such as electrical fittings and hand basins, and to fill the narrow margins around a main field of tiles.

Tile nibblers - a pincer-action tool.

Tools to use

Glazed tiles are relatively easy to cut, because they snap readily along a line scored in the glaze. Cutting unglazed tiles can be tricky, and you may have to buy or hire a special powered saw. Whatever method you adopt, protect your eyes with safety spectacles or goggles when cutting ceramic tiles.

Making straight cuts

It is possible to scribe and snap thin ceramic tiles using just a basic tile scorer and a metal ruler, but the job is made easier with a tile-cutting jig. You can buy inexpensive plastic jigs that you use to guide a hand-held scorer, then snap the tile with a special pincer-action tool; but if you have lots of tiles to cut, invest in a sturdy lever-action jig.

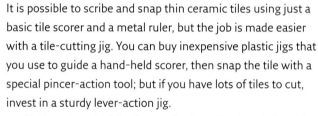

1 Score the line with a smooth stroke.

Mark each end of the line on the face of a glazed tile with a crayon (use a pencil on unglazed tiles), then place the tile against the jig's fence, aligning the marks with the cutting wheel. Push the wheel across the surface to score the glaze (1).

Place the tile in the jig's snapping jaws, aligning the scored line with the arrow marked on the tool, then press down on the lever to snap the tile (2).

Using a powered wet saw

Use a wet saw to cut thick unglazed tiles, and to cut the corner out of tiles that have to fit around an electrical socket or switch. The saw has a diamond-coated blade that runs in a reservoir of water for lubrication and has an adjustable fence that helps

2 Press down on the lever to snap the tile.

make accurate cuts. You can adjust the angle of the blade to mitre thick tiles that meet in a corner. When using this type of saw, tuck in loose clothing and remove any jewellery.

Adjust the fence to align the marked cut line with the blade and tighten the fence clamp. Switch on the saw and feed the tile steadily into the blade, keeping fingers clear of the cutting edge (1). When removing a narrow strip, use a notched stick to push the tile forwards.

You have to make two straight cuts to remove a corner from a tile. Make the shortest cut first, then slowly withdraw the tile from the blade. Switch off and readjust the fence, then make the second cut to remove the waste (2).

1 Feed the tile into the blade.

2 Make a second cut to remove the corner.

Sealing wide gaps

Don't use grout to fill the gap between a tiled wall and a shower tray, bath or basin: a rigid seal can crack and allow water to seep in. Instead, use a flexible silicone sealant to fill gaps up to 3mm (⅛in) wide. Sealant can be clear or come in a range of colours.

Using flexible sealant

With the cartridge fitted into its applicator, trim the tip off the plastic nozzle at an angle (the amount you remove dictates the thickness of the bead).

Clean the surfaces with a paper towel wetted with methylated spirit. Then to apply a bead of sealant, start at one end by pressing the tip into the joint and pull backwards while slowly squeezing the applicator's trigger. When the bed is complete, smooth any ripples by dipping your finger into a 50/50 mix of water and washing-up liquid and running it along the joint. If you have sensitive skin, use the handle of a wetted teaspoon.

Pull back slowly to deposit a bead to sealant.

Fitting other wall tiles

Ceramic tiles are ideal in bathrooms and kitchens where at least some of the walls will inevitably get splashed with water – but in other areas of the home you may decide to use tiles for reasons other than practicality.

Press the sheets onto the adhesive.

Mosaic tiles

When applying mosaic tiles to a wall, use adhesives and grouts as with standard ceramic tiles. Some mosaics have a mesh backing, which is pressed into the adhesive. Others have facing paper which is left on the surface until the adhesive sets.

Fill the main area of the wall, carefully fixing the sheets onto the adhesive. Place an offcut over the sheets and tap with a mallet to bed the tiles into the adhesive. Fill margins by cutting strips from the sheet. Use nibblers to cut individual tiles around awkward shapes. If needs be, soak off the facing paper with a damp sponge, then grout the tiles.

Tap the sheets in lightly using a rubber mallet and an offcut.

Plastic tiles

You can cover a wall relatively quickly with moulded-plastic tiles 300mm (1ft) square. Being backed with expanded polystyrene, they are extremely lightweight and warm to the touch. Plastic tiles are ideal in bathrooms or kitchens where condensation is a problem, but don't hang them in close proximity to cookers or boilers, or even to radiators, as they may soften and distort.

Using guide battens, set out the area to be tiled; then thinly spread the special adhesive supplied by the manufacturer across the back of each tile. Press the tiles firmly against the wall, butting them together gently. Because they are flexible, plastic tiles will accommodate slightly imperfect walls.

Grout the moulded 'joints' with the branded non-abrasive product sold with the tiles. Use a damp sponge to remove surplus grout before it sets hard or clean them afterwards with methylated spirit.

Plastic tiles are easy to shape with a craft knife when fitting around pipework or electrical points.

Cork tiles

Set up a horizontal guide batten to make sure you lay cork tiles accurately. However, it isn't necessary to fix a vertical batten, as the relatively large tiles are easy to align. Simply mark a vertical line centrally on the wall and hang the tiles in both directions from it.

You will need a rubber-based contact adhesive to fix cork tiles (use a glue that allows some movement when positioning the tiles). If any adhesive gets onto the face of a tile, clean it off immediately with the recommended solvent on a cloth.

Spread adhesive thinly and evenly onto the wall and the back of the tiles, and leave it to dry. As you lay each tile, place one edge only against either the batten or the neighbouring tile, holding the rest of it away from the glue-covered wall for the time being. Then gradually lower and press the tile against the wall, and smooth it down with your palms.

Cut cork tiles with a sharp trimming knife. Since the edges are butted tightly, you will need to be very accurate when marking out margin tiles; use the same method as for laying cork and vinyl floor tiles. Cut and fit curved shapes using a template.

Unless the tiles are precoated, apply two coats of varnish after 24 hours.

must know

Fixing mirror tiles
It is difficult to cut glass except in straight lines, so avoid using these in an area which would entail complicated fitting. Mirror tiles are usually fixed close-butted with self-adhesive pads, so no grouting is necessary. Set out the wall with guide battens as for ceramic tiles. Peel the protective paper from the pads and lightly position each tile. Check its alignment with a spirit level, then press it firmly into place, using a soft cloth.

Fitting ceiling tiles

There are two types of tiles you can use on a ceiling – expanded polystyrene and mineral fibre. Polystyrene tiles are the most popular, as they are inexpensive and easy to cut and can be stuck to the ceiling without difficulty. For a more luxurious finish, consider using mineral-fibre tiles.

Stapling mineral-fibre tiles

Mineral-fibre tiles are stapled to softwood battens that are nailed to ceiling joists. Check the direction of the joists by examining the floor above, or by looking in the loft. If lifting floorboards is inconvenient, locate joists from below by tapping the ceiling and listening for a dull thud that indicates the position of a joist. Poke with the bradawl to locate the approximate centre of a couple of joists, then measure from these points – anything from 300 to 450mm (1 to 1ft 6in) apart – and mark their centres on the ceiling plaster.

Marking out the tiles

Start by marking two bisecting lines across the ceiling, so you can work out the spacing of the tiles in order to create even margins.

Mineral-fibre tiles are fixed to a framework of battens nailed to the ceiling at right angles to the joists.
1 Space the battens to match the width of the tiles. Arrange the battens to leave even margins all round.
2 Fix two rows of margin tiles, starting with the corner one.
3 Staple the remaining tiles to the battens, working diagonally across the ceiling.

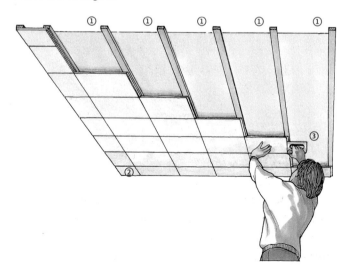

Nailing up the battens

Nail parallel strips of 50 x 25mm (2 x 1in) sawn timber across the ceiling at right angles to the joists, making the distance between batten centres one tile-width.

Stapling the tiles

Begin with the margins. Measure the margin tiles and cut off their tongued edges. Starting with the cut tile in the corner, fix two adjacent rows of margin tiles by stapling through the grooved edges into the battens. Fix their other edges by driving panel pins through their faces. Proceed diagonally across the ceiling by fixing whole tiles into the angle formed by the margin tiles. Slide the tongues of each tile into the grooves of its neighbours, then staple it through its own grooved edge.

Fixing polystyrene tiles

Polystyrene tiles can be used in most rooms in the house except a kitchen, where they would be directly over a source of heat.

Setting out the ceiling

Snap two chalked lines crossing each other at right angles in the centre of the ceiling. Align the first rows of tiles with the lines.

Applying the tiles

Either use a heavy-duty wallpaper paste or a non-flammable contact adhesive for gluing expanded polystyrene. Brush the adhesive evenly across the back of the tiles and onto the ceiling. When the adhesive is touch-dry, align one edge and corner of each tile with one of the right angles formed by the marked lines or another tile, then press the tile against the ceiling.

want to know more?

Take it to the next level...

▶ **Preparing plasterwork** 36–7
▶ **Patching plasterwork** 38–9
▶ **Preparing tiled surfaces** 64–7
▶ **Choosing your floor surfaces** 142–3
▶ **Choosing carpets** 156–9

Other sources...

▶ **Take a professional tiling course. These are available both face-to-face and online. Check out websites such as www.professional-itt.com/pitt for details.**
▶ **Download a heap of valuable tiling tips from www.igoe.ie**
▶ **Try salvage yards for old and unusual tiles to complement a character property.**
▶ **Go to the Ideal Home Exhibition and similar shows for lots of great ceramic tiling ideas.**

6 Floor coverings

A well-decorated room can be enhanced or ruined by its floor covering, which inevitably dominates a large expanse of the living space. Many people make the mistake of not thinking about what should go on the floor until they have finished decorating, by which time they might need to save money or are forced into some sort of unsuitable compromise. Make the floor part of your decorating plans from the outset, and enjoy complementing your walls, windows and ceilings with one of the myriad different materials and textures now available.

Choosing your floor surface

Apart from laying carpet over a floor surface, there are many other coverings from which to choose. Your choice will vary depending on what the room is used for, how much wear the floor is likely to get, and cost and affordability.

Ceramic floor tiles

As with wall tiling, square and rectangular tiles are the most economical ones to buy and lay, but hexagonal and octagonal floor tiles are also available. Tiles with interlocking curved edges require careful setting out in order to achieve a satisfactory result. Choose non-slip, unglazed ceramic tiles for bathrooms and other areas where the floor is likely to become wet.

Quarry tiles

Thick, unglazed quarry tiles are ceramic tiles with a mellow appearance and are among the most durable for floor surfaces. Hand-made quarries are uneven in colour, producing a beautiful mottled effect. Round-edge 'bullnose' quarry tiles can be used as treads for steps; and shaped tiles are available for creating a skirting around a quarry-tile floor.

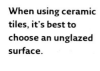

When using ceramic tiles, it's best to choose an unglazed surface.

Stone and slate

A floor laid with natural stone or slate tiles will be exquisite but expensive. Sizes and thicknesses vary according to the manufacturer – some will even cut to measure. These materials are so costly that you should consider hiring a professional to lay them. Consider installing under-floor heating, as the surface is cold under foot, especially in winter.

Vinyl tiles

Vinyl can be cut easily; provided tiles are firmly glued with good butt joints between them, the floor will be waterproof. They are also among the cheapest and easiest floorcoverings to lay. A standard coated tile has a printed pattern sandwiched between a vinyl backing and a harder, clear-vinyl surface.

A selection of stone and slate floor tiles.

Sheet floorcoverings

The most well known sheet floorcovering, particularly in kitchens, must be lino (linoleum). It is extremely hardwearing, comes in many patterns and colours, and is less expensive than other floorcoverings. Depending on the shape of your room, it might be advisable to get a professional to lay the lino, if you do not feel confident in cutting complex shapes into the material.

Sheet vinyl flooring is easier, as it is more pliable and easy to cut. The material is still tough and hardwearing, though; it is more durable depending on the thickness.

Laminate flooring is prized for its practicality and good looks.

Laminate flooring has become increasingly popular in recent years. They are ideal for all ground floor living areas and hallways. However, they aren't recommended for bathrooms or kitchens as the boards may swell if water is regularly spilt on them. Most types of laminates click or slot together in a tongue-and-groove fashion, and so are reasonably easy to lay. Care will need to be taken when cutting non-standard lengths or widths, but most come with detailed manufacturer's instructions.

Setting out soft floor tiles

Soft tiles – such as vinyl, rubber, cork and carpet – are relatively large, so you can cover the floor fairly quickly. Also, they can be cut easily, with a sharp trimming knife or even with scissors, so fitting to irregular shapes isn't difficult.

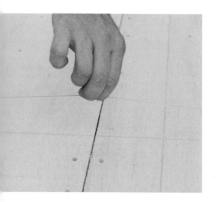

Snap a chalk line between the points.

Marking out the floor

It's possible to lay soft tiles onto either a solid-concrete or a suspended wooden floor, provided the surface is level, clean and dry. Most soft tiles are set out in a similar way: you need to find and mark the centre of the room on the floor. Do this using a chalk line.

Measure and mark the halfway point on opposite walls, then do likewise for the end walls. Next, you just stretch and snap a chalk line between the marks. Where the lines meet in a cross, this is the centre of the room.

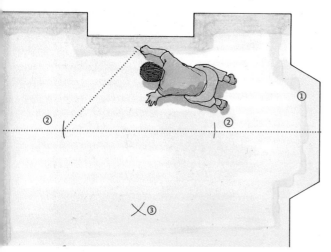

A quartered room ensures that tiles are laid symmetrically.

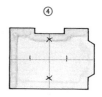

Right angle complete.

Another method is to find the centre of two opposite walls and mark a line across the floor. To draw a line at right angles to the first, using string and a pencil as an improvised compass, scribe arcs on the marked line at equal distances each side of the centre (2). From each point, scribe arcs on both sides of the line (3) that bisect each other. Join the points to form a line across the room (4).

Lay loose tiles at right angles to one of the lines up to one wall. If there's a gap of less than half a tile-width, move the line sideways by half a tile in order to create a wider margin. Nail a guide batten against one line, to help align the first row of tiles.

Diagonal tiling

Arranging tiles diagonally can create an unusual decorative effect, especially if your choice of tiles enables you to mix colours. Setting out and laying the tiles off centre is not complicated – it's virtually the same as fixing them at right angles, except that you will be working towards a corner instead of a straight wall.

Mark a centre line, and bisect it at right angles, using an improvised compass (see previous page for how to do this). Next, draw a line at 45 degrees through the centre point. Dry-lay a row of tiles to plot the margins and mark another line at right angles to the first diagonal. Check the margins as before, making sure they are wide enough. Fix a batten along one diagonal as a guide to laying the first row of tiles.

Diagonal floor tiles.

Laying vinyl floor tiles

Tiles precoated with adhesive can be laid quickly and simply, and there is no risk of squeezing glue onto the surface. If you are not using self-adhesive tiles, follow the tile manufacturer's instructions concerning the type of adhesive to use.

Position a corner of the tile in the centre.

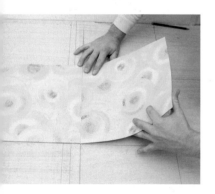

Lay the next tile on the other side of the centre line, abutting the first tile.

Fixing self-adhesive tiles

If you are working with vinyl, take the tiles out of their boxes and leave them stacked up in the room for about 24 hours. This will enable them to be more flexible, thus making them easier to work with.

If the tiles have a directional pattern, make sure you lay them the correct way; some tiles have arrows printed on the back to guide you.

Remove the protective paper backing from the first tile, then press its edge against the guide batten, aligning one corner with the centre line. Gradually lower the tile onto the floor and press it firmly down.

Lay the next tile on the other side of the centre line, butting against the first tile. Form a square with two more tiles. Lay tiles around the square to form a pyramid. Continue in this way to fill one half of the room, but lay only full tiles – leave the margin areas until later on, when you will need to cut tiles. Then remove the batten and tile the other half.

Cutting to fit

Floors are usually out of square, so you have to cut margin tiles to fit the gaps next to the skirting.

Trimming margin tiles

To trim a tile one, lay a loose tile exactly on top of the last full tile. Place another tile on top, but with its edge touching the wall. Draw along the edge of this tile with a pencil, a crayon or a piece of chalk to mark the tile below. Remove the marked tile and cut along the line, then simply glue the cut-off portion of the tile into the margin.

Cutting irregular shapes

To fit curves and mouldings, make a template for each tile out of very thin card or heavy paper. Place the paper template up against the object to reproduce its shape, creasing the template as tightly round the object as you can possibly get it. The next step is to transfer the template to a tile and cut it to shape.

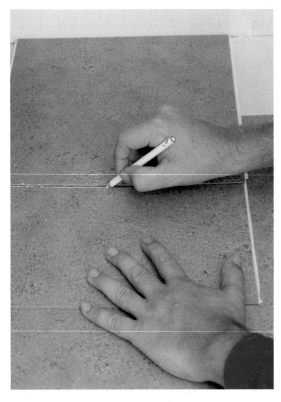

Draw along the edge of the tile against the wall to mark the tile below.

Fitting around pipes

Mark the position of the pipe on the tile, using a compass. Starting from the perimeter of the circle, draw two parallel lines to the edge of the tile. Cut the hole for the pipe, using a home-made punch (see right). Then cut a slit between the marked lines and fold the tile back so you can slide it into place behind the pipe.

Punch holes for pipes with a sharpened offcut.

Laying other soft floor tiles

The procedures for laying floor tiles made from carpet, cork and rubber are similar in many respects to those described opposite for vinyl tiles. The differences are outlined below.

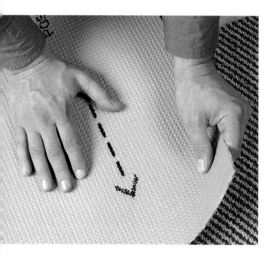

Some carpet tiles have arrows on the back to indicate the direction in which they should be laid.

Carpet tiles

Carpet tiles are laid in the same way as vinyl tiles, except that they are not usually glued down. Set out centre lines on the floor, but don't fit a guide batten – simply aligning the row of tiles with the marked lines is sufficient.

Carpet tiles have a pile that has to be laid in the correct direction. This is sometimes indicated by arrows marked on the back of each tile.

Some tiles have ridges of rubber on the back, so they will slip easily in one direction but not in another. The non-slip direction is also typically denoted by an arrow on the back of the tile. It is usual to lay these tiles in pairs, so one tile can prevent the other from moving.

In any case, stick down every third row of tiles using double-sided carpet tape, and tape all squares in areas where there is likely to be heavy traffic.

Cut and fit carpet tiles as described for vinyl tiles.

Cork tiles

Use a contact adhesive when laying cork tiles: thixotropic adhesives allow a certain degree of movement as you position the tiles. Make sure the tiles are level by tapping down the edges with a small block of wood. Unfinished tiles can be sanded lightly to remove any minor irregularities. Vacuum then seal the unfinished tiles, applying two to three coats of clear varnish.

Rubber tiles

Bed rubber floor tiles onto latex flooring adhesive. Place one edge and corner of each tile against its neighbouring tiles before lowering it onto the adhesive.

Covering a plinth with soft tiles

You can make kitchen base units or a bath panel appear to float above the ground by running floor tiles up the face of the plinth. Hold carpet tiles into a tight bend with gripper strip, but glue other types of soft floor tile in place to create a similar detail.

Glue a plastic moulding (normally used to seal around the edge of a bath) behind the floorcovering to produce a curved detail that will make cleaning the floor a lot easier.

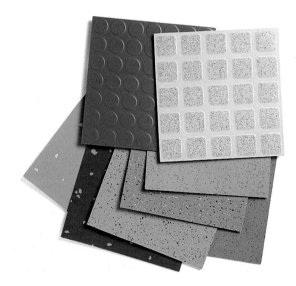

A selection of rubber floor tiles in various colours and textures.

Laying ceramic floor tiles

Ceramic floor tiles make a durable surface that can be extremely decorative. Laying the tiles on a floor is similar to hanging them on a wall – although, being somewhat thicker, floor tiles are generally more difficult to cut.

Setting out

Mark out the floor as for soft floor tiling and work out the spacing to achieve fairly wide even margins. Nail two softwood guide battens to the floor, set at 90 degrees and aligned with the last row of whole tiles on the two adjacent walls farthest from the door. Check the angle by measuring three units from the corner along one batten and four units along the other. Measure the diagonal between the mark – it should measure five units if the battens form a right angle (see below). Make a final check by dry-laying a square of tiles.

Laying the tiles

Use a proprietary floor-tile adhesive that is waterproof and slightly flexible when set. Spread it on in accordance with the adhesive manufacturer's recommendations. Just like wall tiling,

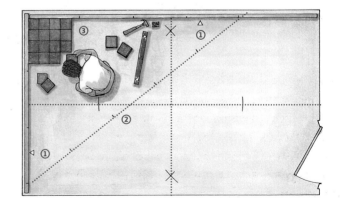

the normal procedure is to apply adhesive to the floor for the main area of tiles, and to butter the backs of cut tiles.

Spread enough adhesive on the floor to cover about 1 sq m (1 sq yd). Press the tiles into the adhesive, starting in the corner. Work along both battens and then fill in between to form the square, using plastic floor-tile spacers to create regular joints.

Apply the adhesive to the floor.

Wipe adhesive off the surface of the tiles with a damp sponge. Then check their alignment with a straightedge, and make sure they are lying flat by checking them with a spirit level. Work your way along one batten, laying one square of tiles at a time; and then tile the rest of the floor in the same way, working back towards the door. Don't forget to scrape adhesive from the margins as you go.

Work your way along the batten.

Allow the adhesive to dry for 24 hours before you walk on the floor to remove the guide battens and fit the margin tiles. Even then, it's a good idea to spread your weight with a board or plank.

Cutting ceramic floor tiles

Fill the gaps between tiles with grouting.

Measure the margin tiles as described for wall tiles, then score and snap them with a tile-cutting jig. Because they are thicker, floor tiles will not snap quite so easily, so you may have to resort to using a powered wet saw – even for simple straight cuts. Seal around the edge of the floor with a dark-coloured flexible sealant.

Laying quarry tiles

Being tough and hardwearing, quarry tiles are an ideal choice for floors that receive heavy use. However, they are relatively thick and making even a straight cut requires a wet saw, so use quarry tiles only in areas that do not require a lot of complex shaping.

must know

Setting out a quarry-tiled floor
Setting out a floor for quarry tiles requires three levelled battens.
1 Fix two guide battens (each about twice the tile thickness) at right angles to one another.
2 Dry-lay 16 tiles in the angle to check its accuracy.
3 Fix the third batten parallel with one of the others, then proceed with tiling.

Correct surface

Don't lay quarry tiles on a suspended wooden floor: replace the floorboards with 18 or 22mm (¾ or ⅞in) exterior-grade plywood to provide a sufficiently flat and rigid base. A concrete floor presents no problems, so long as it is free from damp. You can lay quarries using a floor-tile adhesive, but the traditional method of laying the tiles on a bed of mortar takes care of slightly uneven floor surfaces.

Setting out

Set out two guide battens at right angles to each other in a corner of the room, as described for ceramic floor tiles (see pages 150–1). The depth of the battens should measure about twice the thickness of the tiles, to allow for the mortar bed. Use long

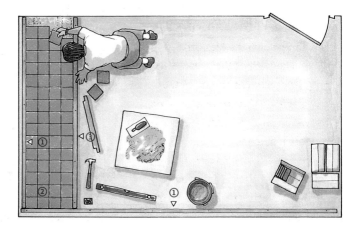

masonry nails to fix them temporarily to a concrete floor. The level of the battens is vital, so check with a spirit level and pack out under the battens with scraps of hardboard or card where necessary. As a guide to positioning, mark tile-widths along each batten, leaving 3mm (⅛in) gaps between them for grouting.

Dry-lay a square of 16 tiles in the angle, then nail a third batten to the floor, butting against the tiles and parallel with one of the other battens. Level and mark it as before.

Mark up margin tiles as for wall tiling and cut them with a powered wet saw.

Laying the tiles

Lay quarry tiles on a bed of mortar made from 1 part cement : 3 parts builder's sand. When water is added, the mortar should be stiff enough to hold an impression when squeezed.

Soak quarry tiles in water prior to laying to prevent them absorbing water from the mortar too rapidly, causing poor adhesion. Cut a stout board to span the parallel battens: this will be used to level the mortar bed and tiles. Cut a notch in each end to fit between the battens; its depth should match the thickness of a tile less 3mm (⅛in).

Spread the mortar to a depth of about 12mm (½in) to cover the area of 16 tiles. Level the mortar by dragging the notched side of the board across it. Dust dry cement on the mortar, then lay the tiles along three sides of the square against the battens. Fill in the square, spacing the tiles by adjusting them with a trowel. Tamp down the tiles gently with the unnotched side of the board until they are level with the battens. If the mortar is too stiff, brush water into the joints. Wipe mortar from the faces of the tiles before it hardens.

Fill in between the battens, then move one batten back to form another bay of the same size. Level it to match the first section.

Tamp down the tiles gently until level.

Wooden flooring

Parquet flooring is a relatively thin covering of decorative timber that is laid in the form of panels or narrow strips. Laminate is a hard surface flooring utilising a fibreboard core and Melamine wear layer that is most often available in planks or sheets.

Preparing the subfloor

Laying any type of parquet or laminate is similar to tiling a floor, but take into consideration the state of the subfloor.

Whether the subfloor is concrete or wood, it must be clean, dry and flat before wooden flooring is laid. Use hardboard panels to level a wooden floor; screed a concrete base. Some manufacturers recommend that a building paper or thin plastic-foam underlay is laid for floating parquetry. To reduce the risk of warping, leave laminate and parquet panels or strips for several days in the room where they will be laid, so they adjust to the atmosphere.

Types of flooring

Parquet floors can be constructed from tongue-and-groove (T&G) or square-edged strips or tiles, either machined from solid timber or made from veneered plywood. They can also come in hardwood panels 450mm (1ft 6in) square. With most forms of parquet flooring, the sections need to be glued to wooden or concrete floors, their edges butted like floor tiles; some types are self-adhesive.

Laminate flooring has become the most popular – and least expensive – method of achieving the look of a real wood floor. Nearly all types of laminate flooring nowadays do not require adhesive; the boards simply click together and just require light tapping to secure a really tight join, so laying is an easier option than with parquet flooring.

Laying laminate flooring

For a softer cushioned tread, lay an underlay over the subfloor. Start laying the laminate boards in the left hand corner of the room, working along the wall. Leave a gap of about 10mm (⅜in) from the wall; use small wedge shapes to help.

Fit the next section by placing the end of the board at an angle and clicking it into place. Carry on in this way until you come to the final board. This will inevitably need to be cut to fit the space. Lay it roughly 10mm (⅜in) from the wall, using wedges or spacers, with its grooved end facing the wall, and mark where it crosses the previous board. Cut to size using a jigsaw. Finally, join the final board together with the previous one and put wedges against the wall.

Continue laying the next row, fitting the boards snugly together. When you reach the final row, lay a loose board directly on top of the penultimate row. Next, place another board, with the tongue side touching the wall, again on top. Using wedges, make the 10mm (⅜in) gap, then mark along the edge of the top board with a pencil onto the board below. Cut the board with a jigsaw.

Once all the boards are laid out, take away all the wedges or spacers and fix a matching beading to the skirting board around the room to cover the gaps.

Roll out the underlay before laying the flooring.

Use wedges or spacers against the skirting.

Press the board at an angle to the first one.

Choosing carpets

Originally, piled carpets were made by knotting strands of wool or other natural fibres into a woven structure; but with machine-made carpets and synthetic fibres, there is a much wider variety. Whether the need is for something luxurious or practical and hardwearing, there is a good choice available for all areas of the house.

Where is it going?

When selecting carpet, consider your options carefully. The floor area is an important element in the style of an interior, and the wrong choice could be an expensive mistake.

A well-laid good-quality carpet will last for many years – so unless you can afford to change your floorcovering every time you redecorate, take care to choose one that you will be able to live with after a change of colour scheme or furnishings. Neutral or earthy colours are easiest to accommodate. Plain colours and small repeat patterns are suitable for rooms of any size; large, bold designs are best reserved for spacious interiors.

If you are planning to carpet adjoining rooms, consider using the same carpet to link the floor areas. This provides a greater sense of space and harmony.

You can use patterned borders in combination with plain carpet to create a distinctive made-to-measure floorcovering in specific areas.

Making your choice

When shopping for carpeting there are various factors to consider, including fibre content, type of pile and durability. Although wool carpet is luxurious, synthetic-fibre carpets also have a lot to offer in terms of finish, texture, comfort underfoot and value for money.

Fibre content

The best carpets are made from wool or a mixture of wool plus a percentage of man-made fibre. Wool carpets are expensive, so manufacturers have experimented with a variety of fibres to produce cheaper but durable and attractive carpets. Materials such as nylon, polypropylene, acrylic, rayon and polyester are all used for carpet making, either singly or in combination.

Synthetic-fibre carpets were once inferior substitutes, often with an unattractive shiny pile and a reputation for building up a charge of static electricity that produced mild shocks when anyone touched a metal door knob. Nowadays, manufacturers have largely solved the problem of static, but you should still seek the advice of the supplier before you buy.

1 Looped pile.
2 Twisted pile.
3 Saxony pile.
4 Underlays.
5 Woven jute.
6 Cord pile.
7 Velvet pile.
8 Cut pile.

Laying carpet

Some people loose-lay carpet, relying on the weight of the furniture to stop it moving around. However, a properly stretched and fixed carpet looks much neater – and, provided you are carpeting a fairly simple rectangular room, is easier than you think.

Fold tacked to floor.

Methods of fixing

There are different methods for holding a carpet firmly in place, depending on the type of carpet you are laying.

Carpet tacks

Double-sided tape.

A 50mm (2in) strip can be folded under along each edge and nailed to a wooden floor with improved cut tacks every 200mm (8in). With this method, the underlay should be laid 50mm (2in) short of the skirting to allow the carpet to lie flat along the edge.

Double-sided tape

Gripper strip.

Use adhesive tape for rubber-backed carpets only. Stick 50mm (2in) tape around the room's perimeter; when you are ready to fix the carpet, peel off the protective paper layer from the tape.

Gripper strips

Double threshold bar.

These wooden or metal strips have fine metal teeth that grip the woven foundation. Nail the strips to the floor, 6mm (¼in) from the skirting, with the teeth pointing towards the wall. Cut short strips to fit into doorways and alcoves. Glue gripper strips to a concrete floor. Cut underlay up to the edge of each strip.

Laying standard-width carpet

Single threshold bar.

If you are laying a separate underlay, join neighbouring sections with short strips of carpet tape or secure them with a few tacks to stop them moving.

Roll out the carpet, butting one machine-cut edge against a wall: fix that edge to the floor. A pattern should run parallel to the main axis of the room.

Stretch the carpet to the opposite wall and temporarily fix it with tacks or slip it onto gripper strips. Work from the centre towards each corner, stretching and fixing the carpet; then do the same at the other sides of the room.

Cut a triangular notch at each corner, so the carpet will lie flat. Adjust the carpet until it is stretched evenly, then fix it permanently. When you are using tape or gripper strips, press the carpet into the angle between the skirting and the floor with a bolster chisel; then trim with a knife held at 45 degrees to the skirting. Tuck the cut edge behind a gripper strip with the bolster.

Carpeting a staircase

If possible, use standard-width narrow carpet on a staircase. Order an extra 450mm (1ft 6in), so that the carpet can be moved at a later date to even out the wear. This allowance is turned under onto the bottom step.

You can fit carpeting across the width of the treads, or stop short to reveal a border of polished or painted wood. With the latter method, you can use traditional stair rods to hold the carpet against the risers; screw brackets on each side of the stairs to hold the rods.

Alternatively, tack the carpet to the stairs every 75mm (3in) across the treads. Push the carpet firmly into the angle between riser and tread with a bolster chisel while you tack the centre, then work outwards to each side.

Unless it's rubber-backed, you can use gripper strip to fix the carpet in place.

Straight stairs
1 Tack underlay pads.
2 Tack carpet face down on first tread.
3 **Pull over nosing and tack to base of riser.**
4 **Run carpet upstairs, fixing to grippers.**

Winding stairs
Don't cut the carpet, but fold the excess under (1) and fix to the risers with stair rods or long carpet tacks.

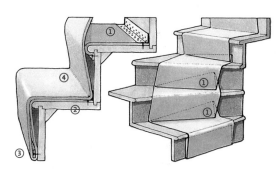

Carpeting a straight run.

Carpeting winding stairs.

Sheet-vinyl floorcovering

Sheet vinyl makes an ideal wall-to-wall floorcovering for kitchens, utility rooms and bathrooms, where you are bound to spill water from time to time. It is straightforward to lay, provided you follow a systematic procedure.

Types of vinyl floorcovering

There are a great many sheet-vinyl floorcoverings to choose from. Make your selection according to durability, colour, pattern and, of course, cost.

Unbacked vinyl

1 Unbacked vinyl.
2 Backed vinyl.
3 Vinyl carpet.

Sheet vinyl is made by sandwiching the printed pattern between a base of PVC and a clear protective PVC covering. All vinyls are relatively hardwearing, but some have a thicker,

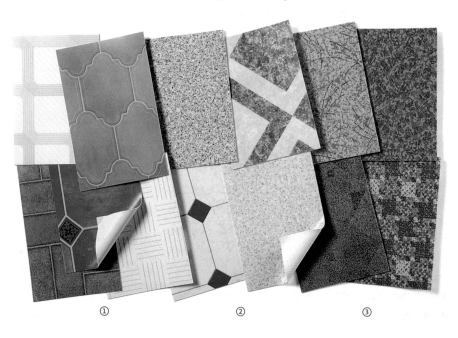

①   ②   ③

reinforced protective layer to increase their durability; ask the supplier which type will suit your needs best.

All varieties of vinyl floorcovering come in a vast range of colours, patterns and textures.

Backed vinyl

Backed vinyl has similar properties to the unbacked type, with the addition of a resilient underlay to make it warmer and softer to walk on. The backing is usually a cushion of foamed PVC.

Vinyl carpet

Vinyl carpet – a cross between carpet and sheet vinyl – was originally developed for contract use in businesses and commerce, but is now available for the wider market, including domestic use. It has a velvet-like pile of fine nylon fibres embedded in a waterproof expanded-PVC base, and is popular for kitchens as spillages are washed off easily with water and a mild detergent. It comes in 2m (6ft 6in) wide rolls.

Sheet-vinyl floorcovering is a popular choice for the kitchen area.

Preparing the floor

Before you lay a sheet of vinyl floorcovering, make sure the floor is flat and dry. Vacuum the surface, and nail down any floorboards that are loose. Take out any unevenness by screeding a concrete floor or hardboarding a wooden one. A concrete floor must have a damp-proof membrane, while a ground-level wooden floor must be ventilated below. Don't lay vinyl over boards that have recently been treated with preserver.

must know

Vinyl flooring
Being hardwearing and waterproof, sheet vinyl is one of the most popular floorcoverings for bathrooms and kitchens. Vinyl carpet has a pile, but is equally suitable for these areas.

Laying sheet vinyl

As with vinyl tiles, leave the vinyl sheet in a room for 24 to 48 hours before laying, preferably opened flat – or at least stood on end, loosely rolled. Make a scribing gauge by driving a nail through a wooden lath about 50mm (2in) from one end. You will use this gauge for fitting the sheet against the skirtings.

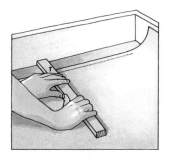

Fit to first wall by scribing with a nailed strip.

Make triangular cuts around a curve.

Fitting and cutting sheet vinyl

Assuming there are no seams, start by fitting the sheet against the longest wall. Pull the vinyl away from the wall by approximately 35mm (1½in); make sure it is parallel with the wall or the main axis of the room. Use the scribing gauge to score a line that follows the skirting. Cut the vinyl with a knife or scissors, then slide the sheet up against the wall.

To get the rest of the sheet to lie as flat as possible, cut a triangular notch at each corner. At external corners, make a straight cut down to the floor. Remove as much waste as possible, leaving 50 to 75mm (2 to 3in) turned up all round.

Using a bolster, press the vinyl into the angle between the skirting and the floor. Align a metal straightedge with the crease and run a sharp knife along it, held at a slight angle to the skirting. If your trimming is less than perfect, nail a cover strip of quadrant moulding to the skirting.

Cutting around a toilet or washbasin

To fit around a WC pan or basin pedestal, fold back the sheet and pierce it with a knife just above floor level; draw the blade up towards the edge of the sheet. Make triangular cuts around the base, gradually working around the curve until the sheet can lie flat on the floor. Crease, and cut off the waste.

Trimming to fit a doorway

Fit the vinyl around the doorframe by creasing it against the floor and trimming off the waste. Make a straight cut across the opening, and fit a threshold bar over the edge of the sheet.

Sticking and joining sheet vinyl

Modern sheet-vinyl floorcoverings can be loose-laid, but you may prefer to at least glue the edges, especially across a door opening.

Peel back the edge and spread a band of the recommended flooring adhesive, using a toothed spreader; or apply double-sided adhesive tape, 50mm (2in) wide, to the floor.

Joining strips of vinyl

If you have to join widths of vinyl, then overlap the free edge with the second sheet until the pattern matches exactly. Cut through both pieces with a knife, then remove the waste strips.

Without moving the sheets so as to keep them properly aligned, fold back both cut edges, apply tape or adhesive, then press the join together.

want to know more?

Take it to the next level...

▶ **Colour schemes** 19-21
▶ **Repairing concrete** 34-5
▶ **Sanding a wooden floor** 46-7
▶ **Using sanding machines** 48-9
▶ **Levelling a wooden floor** 51-3

Other sources...

▶ **Large carpet retail chains such as Allied Carpets and Carpetright are generally happy to discuss carpet schemes and fitting options.**
▶ **Books on interior design from your local library or bookshop can be a great source of inspiration when it comes to floor coverings.**
▶ **Typing the words 'floor coverings' into Google or any other internet search engine throws up a huge array of websites dedicated to the subject.**

7 Decorative effects

In this final chapter, we consider a number of different decorative effects that can be easily and inexpensively applied to walls, ceilings, floors and furniture. These can add an extra dimension to a room and are a great way of personalizing your living space. As well as paint effects from stencilling to crackle glazing, the following pages offer advice on how to apply textured finishes and create decorative mouldings that will brighten the barest room.

Materials and tools

Although you will probably never consider using all the various special effects mentioned in this chapter, it is worthwhile knowing what certain tools and materials are used for.

Standard equipment

Solvents

Solvents are used to dilute or 'thin' paints, to make them easier to work or to reduce their opacity.

Paintbrushes

Decorator's brushes, ranging from 25 to 150mm (1 to 6in), will meet most needs. For fine work, supplement these with a selection of artist's paintbrushes.

There are special textured roller sleeves that allow you to produce large areas of different effects quickly.

Special-effects brushes

Special brushes are used to manipulate the glaze and create different effects. Long-bristle brushes, known as dragging brushes and floggers, make linear marks and wood-grain effects.

Rollers

Rollers are ideal for applying an even coat of paint to large areas. Have a 225mm (9in) medium-pile roller for the main areas and a 100mm (4in) roller for narrow strips. Special rollers are made for creating rag or sponge effects.

Painting accessories

Various containers, such as a paint kettle and screw-top jars, will come in handy, as will old plates to use as palettes for mixing colours. Protect the floor with dust sheets, and use

masking tape to create hard-edge effects.
When working, wear coveralls, rubber gloves and
a face mask.

Stamps and stencils

Stamps and stencils are used to apply a decorative
motif or to make a repeat pattern on a painted
surface. Buy ready-made designs or make your own.

Sponges

Sponges can be used to create random
stippled effects or paint stencils onto
surfaces.

Paints and glazes

Broken-colour decorative effects are
based on a two-part paint system. The
first layer is a basecoat of opaque paint,
usually an eggshell finish or satin vinyl
emulsion. Matt emulsion paints are too

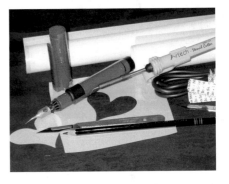

absorbent. White paint is often used as a base for pale shades or
as a background to brightly coloured finishes. Coloured basecoats
are also used to create more vibrant schemes.

**Stencilling is a great
way to individualise
your decorating.**

When the basecoat is dry, a top coat of semi-transparent
coloured glaze (also called scumble) is applied, and then textured
using a variety of techniques. Traditional solvent-based paints
and glazes are available, but water-based acrylic materials dry
faster and are practically odourless.

Colour choice

Make your own colours by tinting white emulsion paint or glaze
medium with pigments, stainers or artist's paints, but it is more
convenient to choose colours from one of the many ready-made
ranges. Paint suppliers can also make up whichever tint you wish.

Changing trends

In recent years there has been a resurgence of interest in using paint to create decorative effects. When applied to walls, ceilings, floors, joinery and furniture – in fact any surface to which paint will adhere – these treatments add individuality to a colour scheme.

Changing fashions

There is a vast range of special effects paints now available, giving many different finishes – metallic or pearlised, for example. And the trend is for home decorators to experiment with creative effects in their own homes. Not only are the effects unique and one-off, but the finishes can add richness and character to your home. Wood graining, gilding and stencilling are just some of the more popular techniques. Others include stippling, metallic paints, colour washing, sponging, rag rolling, masking straight lines on a wall, stamping and dragging.

Some effects will stay in fashion; others will be popular for a year or so, then seem dated for many years after. If you're unsure of what look to go for, spend time looking through the latest home style magazines and paint catalogues before you start to give you an idea of what might suit you – and especially your style of home.

Stencilling can be incorporated into the design of a room to give a spectacular effect.

Painting in various pearlised colours can add vibrancy to a tired piece of furniture, giving it a contemporary look.

Prepare properly

As with any successful paint job, careful preparation is key, which means not just surface preparation but also having the right tools, using the right paint and making sure you have enough for the job in hand.

Mask surfaces with decorator's tape. Decorator's tape is designed to be kind on painted surfaces and should not remove existing paint, which masking tape may do.

Practise first

Although many of the techniques are easy to master, it is worth practising on a piece of board before you tackle an entire room. The texture of the wall itself may influence the finished effect, but at least you will be familiar with the basic techniques. If after painting one or two walls, you decide the result is not to your liking, don't worry – you can always paint over it.

Furniture effects

Decorative effects does not just have to apply to your walls. Furniture that has seen better days can be given a new look by painting it with metallic paint or made to look antique and distressed for a more rustic, care-worn appearance.

Character furniture

If you are looking for elegant, antique furniture but simply cannot afford its price tag, there is an alternative. Using the latest decorative techniques, furniture can be transformed in a matter of hours, creating a time-worn look.

Distressed paintwork

As painted furniture ages, colours mellow and fade and vulnerable areas become worn and scratched. The distressed technique simply recreates this look, such as the example of the kitchen dresser on the left. This appearance of age was achieved on newly painted woodwork.

To achieve this look, lightly rub the paintwork with light grade abrasive paper. Paint a top coat over the piece of furniture and let it dry. Then rub through to the underlying colour using medium-grade abrasive paper.

Alternatively, take an old piece of furniture, thoroughly sand it down and give it a base colour. Once dry, paint a contrasting colour on top and when that is dry, gently sand to reveal the undercoat in patches for a distressed look.

Dragging

Dragging the paint gives a more controlled linear effect. The brushmarks are usually applied vertically, but they can be run horizontally. Apply the special-effect paint or scumble glaze with a roller in even bands. Using a dry dragging brush, or wide paintbrush held at a low angle to the surface, draw the bristles through the wet paint in one continuous stroke from top to bottom. Wipe off excess paint, then repeat the process alongside the first stripe. Continue along the surface, blending in the edges while they are still wet. You can also use a corrugated comb for a more prominent effect.

Decorative paint effects, such as dragging, can brighten up an old item of furniture.

Crackle glaze

The appearance of age can be further enhanced using products that make furniture look discoloured and chipped.

Traditional oil-based paints and varnishes dry out over time and crack. This typical ageing effect can be recreated with crackle glaze, crackle varnish and craquelure.

Sand the surface of the piece of furniture. Apply a base coat of crackle glaze or craquelure using a soft brush. Once dry it becomes clear, remaining slightly tacky. Then apply a topcoat and as it dries fine cracks appear.

To produce an even more authentic aged effect, rub raw umber oil paint into the cracks with a soft cloth and polish off.

Stencilled effects

You can paint patterns or motifs onto walls and furniture, using ready-made paper or plastic stencils. They are available from specialist shops, on the internet and some artists' suppliers.

Paints

You can buy small pots of acrylic paint for stencilling, but water-based stencil paints or ordinary emulsion paint are fine for most projects. Stencil crayons are also available but they are oil based, so they have a longer drying time.

Brushes

Unless you intend to spray paint from an aerosol, you will need a sponge or a special stencil brush that has short stiff bristles and is used with a stippling action. Use a separate brush for each colour, unless you want to spend time cleaning during the project, and choose brushes that are appropriate for the hole sizes of your stencil.

Securing the stencil

Lightly mark out the wall to help position the stencil accurately. At the same time, make small marks to indicate the position of repeat patterns. Use small pieces of masking tape to hold the stencil on the wall, or spray the back of the stencil with a low-tack adhesive.

Use a stippling
motion to put the
motif on the ceiling.

Applying the paint

Take a stencil brush and touch the tips of the bristles into the
paint. Stipple excess paint onto waste paper until it deposits
paint evenly. Use a sponge in a similar way.

With the stencil held flat against the wall, stipple the edges
of the motif first, then fill in the centre. If necessary, apply a
second coat immediately, to build up the required depth of
colour. When the motif is complete, carefully peel the stencil
away from the wall. Wipe traces of paint from the back of the
stencil before repositioning it to repeat the motif.

If paint has crept under the stencil, try dabbing it off with a
piece of absorbent paper rolled into a thin tapered coil, and then
touch in with background paint.

Sealing

Stencils in wet areas or on walls that need wiping over require
protection if your design is to last. Floor stencils and those on
furniture will need protection wherever they are. Use
transparent acrylic varnish when your design is dry. Buy in a flat
(matt) finish so you don't end up with a shiny surface.

Other paint effects

The rise in the number of television programmes showing us how to transform our homes has lead to an increase in the different decorating effects that can be achieved using relatively inexpensive tools and materials.

Above: Metallic paints in various stripes painted on artist's canvases accentuate a plain wall. Opposite: Be bold, with funky, slightly irregular floral patterns to form a harmonious group of shapes. Easy to achieve with some masking tape.

Paint power

Metallic and pearlised paints have become widely available and are excellent for adding a touch of drama to painted walls, items of furniture and canvases. There are no rules as to how and where you should use them. You will find that the look will change depending on light reflections during the day and under artificial light at night the colours will dazzle in spectacular fashion.

There are many other stylish paint effects that have recently been introduced to the market. For instance, interior paint that is designed to produce a suede-effect finish; a modern-looking glimmer-effect paint that leaves walls with a soft shimmer; plus various other ranges that give a translucent, pearlescent mother-of-pearl look to the finished wall. Some of these specialised paints require two applications, often using a different type of brush or paint applicator for each coat so that a particular effect is achieved.

Different techniques, such as rag rolling, sponging, distressing or marbling, can also be used with these specialised paints to create an even wider range of effects.

Contrasting colours next to each other, and especially painted in extraordinary shapes and

Gilding can brighten up any dull surface.

designs, will create powerful, bold effects without the need for any special-effects paint or stains. Remember – don't be afraid to experiment.

Gilding and glass frosting

Gilding is the act of applying gold or silver leaf onto most surfaces, including wood, leather, metal, plastic or glass. The materials needed can be purchased from most arts and crafts supply stores. The leaf generally is sold in books, powders, rolls or transfers, and is carefully brushed onto the surface.

Glass can be given a new look by simply spraying with a frosting spray. You can also buy ready-made etched transfers which you can rub straight onto the surface.

Staining

Use a preservative and stain mixture to add colour to panelling.

Colour stain a bathroom panel or surrounds by using a preservative and stain mixture. Use either a spirit-based preservative or a water-based one. Simply stir the mixture before applying two coats to the surface. If you want a more 'washed out' look, just apply one coat, then dip a clean cloth in some white spirit and gently rub over the surface before the stain dries.

Textured coatings

Textured coatings can be obtained as a dry powder for mixing with warm water or in a ready-mixed form for direct application from the tub. They are available in a range of standard colours, but if none of them suits your decorative scheme you can use ordinary emulsion as a finish.

Choose your texture

Using rollers, scrapers or improvised tools, you can produce a variety of textures. It's advisable to restrict distinctly raised textures with sharp edges to areas where you are unlikely to rub against the wall. Create finer textures for children's rooms, small bathrooms and narrow hallways.

Preparation for textured coatings

New surfaces will need virtually no preparation, but joints between plasterboard must be reinforced with tape. Strip any wallcoverings and key gloss paint with glasspaper. Old walls and ceilings must be clean, dry, sound and free from organic growth. Treat friable surfaces with stabilizing solution.

Although large cracks and holes must be filled, a textured coating will conceal minor defects in walls and ceilings by filling small cracks and bridging shallow bumps and hollows.

Masking joinery and fittings

Use masking tape 50mm (2in) wide to cover doorframes and window frames, electrical fittings, plumbing pipework, picture rails and skirting boards. Lay dust sheets over the floor.

Pat the coating with a damp sponge to create a pitted, stippled finish.

Use a toothed spatula to create a pattern of arcs.

A roller with grooves creates geometric patterns.

Twist a damp sponge to produce random swirls on the wall.

Applying the coating

You can apply the coating, using a roller or broad wall brush, but finer textures are possible with the brush. Buy a special roller if recommended by the coating manufacturer.

With a well-loaded roller, apply a generous coat in a band 600mm (2ft) wide across the ceiling or down a wall. Don't press too hard, and vary the angle of the stroke.

If you decide to brush the coating on, don't spread it out like paint. Instead, lay it on with one stroke and spread it back again with one or two strokes only.

Texture the first band, then apply a second band and blend them together before texturing the latter. Continue in this way until the wall or ceiling is complete. Keep the room ventilated until the coating has hardened.

Painting around fittings

Use a small paintbrush to fill in around electrical fittings and along edges, trying to copy the texture used on the surrounding wall or ceiling. Some people prefer to form a distinct margin around fittings by drawing a small paintbrush along the perimeter to give a smooth finish.

Creating a texture

You can experiment with a variety of tools to make any number of textures. Try a coarse expanded-foam roller or one made with a special surface to produce diagonal or diamond patterns. Alternatively, apply a swirling, ripple or stipple finish with improvised equipment, as shown on the left.

Decorative mouldings

Interior – or architectural – mouldings are available in wood or plaster and include skirting boards, dado rails, picture rails, architrave and cornice mouldings. You may want to reinstate decorative features of this kind if they have been stripped out of an older house or add them to give a new look to a room.

Skirtings

Architectural mouldings are primarily functional, but they also contribute to the visual style and proportion of a room. A relatively tall skirting acts as a base to the composition, similar to the base of a classical column. Pick a moulding to suit the house style.

Dado rails

The dado rail – or chair rail – is a reference to the waist-high dado panelling of earlier times. It provides a strip to protect the wall finish from chair backs and forms a border for textured wallcoverings – typically found in Victorian and Edwardian houses.

Picture rails

Like the dado moulding, the picture rail is an echo from the earlier panelled walls. It is usually set about 300 to 500mm (1ft to 1ft 8in) below the ceiling cornice to form a frieze. Picture-rail mouldings have a groove in the top edge to hold metal hooks for hanging pictures.

1 **Bolection mould skirting.**
2 **Torus skirting. 3 Ovolo skirting.**
4 **Torus/ovolo reverse skirting.**
5 **Bevelled/rounded reverse skirting. 6 Bevelled hardwood skirting.**

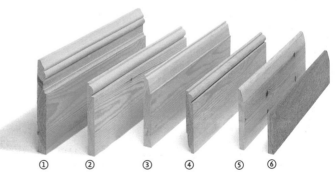

① ② ③ ④ ⑤ ⑥

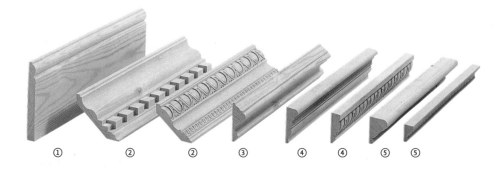

① ② ② ③ ④ ④ ⑤ ⑤

1 **Torus skirting.**
2 **Cornice mouldings.**
3 **Straight-run dado rails.**
4 **Carved dado mouldings.**
5 **Small dado mouldings.**

Cornice mouldings

Cornice mouldings form a bold decorative feature where the walls of a room meet the ceiling. These mouldings are usually made from plaster, but are sometimes made from wood. Ornate mouldings are made in standard lengths with pre-mitred external and pre-scribed internal corner pieces. The mouldings are either bonded or screwed in place.

Architrave

An architrave moulding provides a decorative frame to a door, as well as concealing the joint between the door lining and the wall. Similar mouldings are used around sliding-sash windows. Standard architrave mouldings are stocked by DIY stores and timber merchants, but more elaborate mouldings can be obtained from specialist joinery suppliers.

If there's a particular, more complicated, profile you want to replicate, you can have all your mouldings machined to that pattern by a specialist mouldings maker.

Above left: The two top corners need to be cut at a 45 degree angle (mitred).
Above right: Always check the alignment with a spirit level.

Plaster ceiling roses

Replace an original ceiling moulding that is beyond repair with one of the excellent reproduction mouldings made from fibrous plaster.

If there is a light fitting attached to the ceiling, turn off the power supply at the mains, disconnect and remove the entire fitting. Chip away the old damaged moulding back to the ceiling plaster. Make good the surface with plaster, then leave it to dry.

To determine the exact centre of the ceiling, stretch lengths of string from corner to corner diagonally: where they cross is the centre. Mark the centre point and drill a hole for the lighting cable. If the new centrepiece lacks a hole for a lighting cable, drill one through its centre.

Apply a ceramic-tile adhesive to the back of the moulding, then pass the cable through the hole in the centre and press the moulding firmly into place. On a flat ceiling, suction should be sufficient to hold the moulding, but as a precaution prop it until the adhesive sets.

Reinforce larger plaster mouldings with brass screws driven into the joists above. Always be careful not to disturb existing cable or pipe work when you are doing this. Wipe away surplus adhesive from around the edges of the moulding with a damp brush or sponge.

When the adhesive has set, attach the light fitting. You may need longer screws than previously in order to make a really secure fixing.

want to know more?

Take it to the next level...

▶ **Colour schemes** 19-21
▶ **Types of paint** 70-77
▶ **Applying paint** 87-91
▶ **Choosing tiles** 126-9
▶ **Choosing carpets** 156-9

Other sources...

▶ **Talk to the experts at the Crown Paint Talk helpline for advice and tips about applying decorative effects.**
▶ **Use Crown and Dulux colour cards - available from all good DIY stores - to help promote an understanding of which colours and effects work well together.**
▶ **Contact the Rohm and Haas Paint Quality Institute for further ideas. Their contact details can be found at www.paintquality.co.uk**
▶ **For all sorts of advice about stencils and stencilling, go to www.stencil-library.com**

Glossary

Acrylic
Fast drying, water based paint. A synthetic polymer used in high-performance latex or water-based paints.

Adhesion
The ability of dry paint to remain on the surface without blistering, flaking or cracking. Adhesion is probably the single most important property of paint.

Aggregate
Silicon particles added to paint to produce a coarse finish, usually on exterior work.

Airless spraying
Process of atomization of paint by forcing it through an orifice at high pressure.

Anaglypta
A type of wallpaper made from the pulp of cotton fibre. It is a trade name but is now used to refer to any type of paper with embossed patterns that can be painted.

Antiquating
Artificially ageing a painted surface.

Architrave
Provides a decorative frame to a door, as well as concealing the joint between the door lining and the wall

Arris
The external edge of two surfaces, especially wood and panel-doors.

Artex
A textured finish commonly applied to ceilings. It can be patterned in different ways by combing to create a variety of patterns.

Badger
A very soft brush made from badger hairs used for smoothing lines in graining and varnishing.

Binder
The binder cements the pigment particles into a uniform paint film and also makes the paint adhere to the surface.

Bleaching
Loss of colour, usually caused by exposure to sunlight.

Blow-lamp
A gas or paraffin-oil fuelled blow-torch. Used for burning off old paint.

Blistering
The formulation of dome-shaped, hollow projections on paint, often caused by heat or moisture.

Boxing
Mixing paint for a large area to ensure even shade.

Brown bagging
A decorative technique applied by sticking torn pieces of brown paper bags onto walls, etc.

BSI
British Standards Institute.

Burning-off
A means of removing old paint and varnish, with either a heat-gun or a blowtorch (blowlamp).

BWF
British Woodworking Federation.

Capstan
Undiluted paint used straight from the container.

Casing wheel
A small wheel on a handle used to cut lining papers especially.

Caulk
Flexible filler in tubes.

Ceiling texture
Usually known as artex in the UK. A textured finish with a wide variety of patterns.

China-wood oil
A drying medium. Also called tung oil or wood-oil.

Cladding
Boarding, usually horizontal, on the outside of a building.

Colourwashing
A technique of coating wood with a water-based paint and then removing most of the paint with a cloth thereby exposing the grain. Also used on walls to give a semi-opaque finish.

Comb
Toothed tool used mainly for wood graining.

Cornice
Moulded coving round the edge of a ceiling.

Coving
Ready made cornice generally fixed with adhesive.

Creosote
A wood preservative for exterior fencing, etc.

Crossline
Fixing strips of lining paper horizontally.

Dado
The lower part of a wall decorated differently.

Dado rail
The wooden or plaster moulding designating the top edge of the dado.

Découpage
Decorating a surface using delicate paper cut-outs and lacquer.

Distressing
Treating surfaces so they look old and worn, especially wood.

Drop
A length of wallpaper cut to wall height ready for pasting.

Efflorescence
Powdery residue coming out of stonework onto the painted surface.

Eggshell
A shiny satin type of finish.

Emulsion
A water-based paint known as latex in the USA.

Enamel
Topcoat which is characterized by its ability to form a smooth surface.

Etch
To wear away or roughen a surface with an acid or other chemical agent or with a fine abrasive prior to painting to increase adhesion.

Fading
Lightening of the paint's colour, usually caused by exposure to light or heat.

Fascia
Externally, the board on the ends of rafters usually carrying the guttering (rain trough).

Filler
Comes as a ready-mixed paste or in powder form and is used for repairing small holes and cracks in the surface to be decorated.

Fitch
A small long handled brush used for intricate work.

Flat
A large brush used for ceilings or walls. Also called a distemper brush.

Floor paint
A specialized finish which can be matt, gloss, non-slip, rubberised, cement-based, etc.

French polish
Shellac dissolved in industrial alcohol for use on furniture and high-quality wood finishes.

Fresco
Applying thin water paint to still wet plaster.

Gibroc
Ready made plaster shapes, especially coving.

Glasspaper
Abrasive paper used in preparation work.

Glass paint
A paint used specially for window panes, mirrors, etc.

Glazing
Applying transparent or translucent coatings over a painted surface to produce blended effects of their colours.

Glider
A thin flat brush for applying varnishes.

Gloss paint
The shiny finish coat of paint.

Gold leaf
Leaves of hammered out very thin gold for gilding.

Grisaille
Monochrome painting used to create special effects using elaborate shading technique.

Heat-gun
An electric blow-torch for safely burning off paint.

Hessian
A coarse fabric wallcovering in common use.

Imitation marble
Technique used on all surfaces to give appearance of marble.

Inlay
A decorative technique used in furniture design. Small holes are gouged out of the wooden carcass and materials inserted flush against the wood to make a pattern.

Inset
Recessed panel in a door.

Intumescent coatings
Fire retardant coating.

Jojoba
Liquid wax from the jojoba tree.

Kite mark
Stamp of approval of the BSI. (British Standards Institute).

Knotting
A sealer used on knots in softwoods to prevent resin bleeding through the paint.

Lacquer
Transparent protective film. Can be matt, gloss or eggshell.

Lead paint
No longer allowed as it is highly toxic, but is still found on old paintwork.

Linseed oil
Linseed oil is the general term for the oil extracted from flax seed.

Manilla paper
An oiled paper used to make stencils.

Mastic
Commercially made compound used for sealing joints.

Mastic gun
The applicator for tubes of mastic, decorator's caulk, gripfill, etc. Usually referred to simply as a 'gun'.

Mural
Wall painting.

Non-slip paint
A paint for floors. Floor paint can be applied with a large roller.

Oil paint
A non water-based paint, containing oils and resin. Can be diluted with turpentine.

Opacity
Covering power of paint.

Paper tiger
A device used to scratch wallpaper prior to soaking.

Plumbline
Length of string with weight attached, for checking vertical lines.

Primer
The first coat of paint applied to a surface.

Putty knife
A narrow metal bladed knife used for glazing etc.

Quarry-red
A deep brick red.

Quill
Long feather used for delicate paint touches.

Quirk
A groove or channel in a moulding.

Rag-rolling
A method of producing decorative broken-colour effects by rolling a piece of crumpled fabric or paper over the wet surface of a glaze or distemper.

Rail
Horizontal bars in framing, panelling, etc.

Rebate
A rectangular recess in the edge of a substance enabling it to fit into another piece, thereby forming a joint.

Roller
Used for applying paint, often emulsions.

Sable
Very high quality brush. Often used in signwriting and fine detailed work.

Sander
A tool or machine used for smoothing surfaces.

Sandpaper
An abrasive paper used for smoothing surfaces.

Scraper
A stiff bladed knife used for general preparation work and paint stripping.

Seam roller
A small wooden or plastic roller for use on wallpaper edges.

Spattering
Droplets of paint that spin or mist off the roller as paint is being applied. The application of droplets of paint to obtain a Spatter finish.

Stencil
A paper cut-out, or to produce a pattern or design with a paper cut-out.

Stripper
A chemical compound, in jelly or liquid form used to remove old or damaged paint.

Stucco
A coarse finishing material for walls and wood, often to hide imperfections.

Sugar soap
A caustic soap very effective at removing grease and dirt from paintwork.

Thinners
A liquid added to paints, emulsions, latex etc to reduce their consistency so they may be more easily applied.

Turps
Wood turpentine or turpentine substitute, a solvent used to thin oil paints and clean brushes. Equivalent of White Spirit.

Undercoat
Matt finish paint (usually oil paint) used before the finish coat.

Varnish
A clear finish in either matt, gloss or satin finish. Usually a translucent liquid, which, when applied to a surface in a thin film, dries to a hard and more or less transparent finish.

Water-based
Solvent free paint preparations.

Wet and dry
An fine abrasive sandpaper normally used with clean water to produce a very smooth surface.

White spirit
Used to thin oil paints and clean brushes. Slightly cheaper than turpentine substitute.

Yacht varnish
An extremely durable exterior varnish.

Yellowing
The discolouration of white finishes due to heat, ageing or smoke/fumes.

Need to know more?

Listed below are just some of the websites, books and magazines available to aid you further in accumulating knowledge about painting and decorating, as well as a couple of professional organizations which you can trust to help you if you get in a fix.

Painting and decorating websites

www.askthebuilder.com
www.bbc.co.uk/homes/diy
www.crownpaints.co.uk
www.decoratingdirect.co.uk
www.diy.com
www.diydoctor.org.uk
www.diyfixit.co.uk
www.diynot.com
www.igoe.ie
www.niceic.org.uk/consumers/tips.html
www.paintquality.co.uk
www.professional-itt.com/pitt
www.sandtex.co.uk
www.stencil-library.com
www.thehouseplanner.co.uk
www.wallpapers-uk.com

Books

Collins Complete DIY Manual, Albert Jackson & David Day (HarperCollins)
Fix It Manual, Albert Jackson (HarperCollins)
Tommy Walsh Bathroom DIY, Tommy Walsh (HarperCollins)
Tommy Walsh Kitchen DIY, Tommy Walsh (HarperCollins)
Tommy Walsh Living Spaces DIY, Tommy Walsh (HarperCollins)
Tommy Walsh Outdoor DIY, Tommy Walsh (HarperCollins)

Magazines

BBC Good Homes
(BBC)
Country Homes & Interiors
(IPC Media)
Elle Decoration
(The Magazine Group)
Fine Homebuilding
(The Taunton Press)
Good Housekeeping
(National Magazine Company)
Grand Designs
(Channel 4)
Home DIY
(Highbury Leisure)
House Beautiful
(National Magazine Company)
Ideal Home
(Daily Mail Group)
Practical Householder
(Nexus Media)
The English Home
(The Magazine Group)

Painting and decorating organizations

Visit www.qualitymark.org.uk to find a reputable and trustworthy tradesman in your area who is a member of the government-backed Quality Mark Scheme.

Visit www.bozzle.com for a general list of services.

Index

◌ **Collins** need to know?

Look out for these recent titles in Collins' practical and accessible need to know? series.

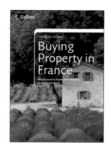

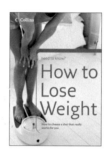

Other titles in the series:

Birdwatching
Body Language
Card Games
DIY
Dog Training
Drawing & Sketching
Golf
Guitar

Kama Sutra
Knots
Pilates
Speak French
Speak Italian
Speak Spanish
Stargazing
Watercolour

Weddings
Wood-Working
The World
Yoga
Zodiac Types

To order any of these titles, please telephone 0870 787 1732. For further information about all Collins books, visit our website: www.collins.co.uk